SHIFT
Church in the 21st Century

Steve White

Shift: Church in the 21st Century
© 2019 Steve White

ISBN-13: 978-0-578-55216-3

Contents

Preface 4

Section One 7

Founding the Church 11

Being the Church 29

Understanding the Times 45

Section Two 59

Paradigm Shift 63

Generational Shift 87

Priority Shift 109

Section Three 127

Embracing our Responsibility 129

Equipping People 143

Engaging Society 171

Conclusion 191

Endnotes 195

Preface

As a parent, pastor, and consultant, I've grown increasingly concerned about leading God's people in a rapidly changing, increasingly antagonistic culture. I don't want to be one of those leaders who proclaim to have all the answers, and then proceed to describe how things used to work. For better or worse, the church used to play a pivotal role in American culture. Sadly, or not, gone are the days when people automatically turn to the church for help in times of crisis. Gone are the days when good programming and good preaching are all that are needed to draw people to the church, and more importantly to the Gospel. The church in North America is in trouble, and it does not yet fully realize the extent of that trouble.

The whole thing started with my personal, pastoral concern about how the church should be responding to the reality that for a number of years, both secular and Christian scholars, preachers and authors have discussed the notion that America is now a post-Christian nation. Research by organizations such as the Pew Center and Barna Group have shown that an increasing number of Americans describe themselves as having no religious affiliation. Study after study shows that our society views the church as irrelevant at best, downright harmful at worst. It wasn't that long ago that Joy Behar, on ABC's *The View*, likened Vice-president Mike Pence's Christian faith to a mental illness. She apologized several weeks later and shortly after that announced her resignation from the show. Still, her ill-advised commentary on Christianity was heard by a worldwide audience, many of whom are beginning to wonder if Behar isn't on to something. Maybe the church really is simply an anachronism, a nod to a bygone era, embraced by those who fear contemporary truth.

As I've read thousands of pages from articles, books, and blogs, spent uncounted hours in conversation with leaders, pastors and others inside and outside the church, taught seminars and facilitated discussion, I've recognized a disturbing theme. Too often we are quick to defend the existing church systems and blame a godless culture. Or perhaps more disturbingly, we boldly attack the church for its failure to respond to that same culture. Neither approach is helpful.

The church in America is organized physically and philosophically around a set of cultural assumptions that are no longer valid. The vast majority of our programming and teaching is designed to address the issues of the America that existed about 50 years ago. One reason our society increasingly views the church as irrelevant is because, quite frankly, we are irrelevant. I know, that was a very strong statement. It's not that the Gospel isn't relevant; it's not that discipleship has no place; it's that our approach is no longer meaningful to massive numbers of people. As a very easy example: most churches still hand out paper bulletins to people who are deeply concerned about waste and the ecological impact of deforestation. In our efforts to be helpful, we inadvertently send a negative message to our guests as soon as they walk in the door. In the 21st century it's hard to talk meaningfully about the Genesis mandate to steward the earth when we're using reams of paper to tell people what's easily found on our web site.

If the church is going to regain its relevance, we need to do more than tweak a few programs, or repaint the lobby, or even find younger pastors who can preach with "freshness and relevance" (yes, churches are doing that). It doesn't matter how young, fresh and relevant the pastor is. If the church as a whole is a memorial to what once was, it will continue to miss the mark in a culture dying for truth, hope and purpose (even if most of that culture doesn't realize it). If the church is going to regain its relevance, we need to start with the basics. What does the Bible say about the nature of the church? What does the Bible say about expectations for how a church goes about fulfilling its purpose? How do we take that information and create an organization that will vehemently hold to the truth of Scripture, while adapting programs and teaching to be meaningful in a rapidly changing culture?

Truthfully, this book raises more questions than it answers. I'm all right with that. Both the questions and the answers in here were sparked from my own desire to be a better parent, more effective pastor, and relevant consultant. I've found that even asking the questions with humility and sincerity has helped in all those areas. I pray even if only because of the questions, this will also help you lead with relevance and effectiveness in your own sphere of influence.

Section One

Much of the church in America is frantically trying to figure out what went wrong. Attendance is declining in both quantity and quality as fewer people attend, and those who do attend do so less frequently. Traditional church growth and outreach approaches are seeing slower and smaller responses as culture shifts. People think in new ways, have a different set of priorities and don't seem to be drawn to the church or the Gospel as they once were.

The church finds itself scrambling to regain a lost sense of ... something; scrambling to figure out why people don't respond the way they used to; scrambling to refresh programs and policies that have worked for many, many years. Yet the more we scramble, the harder we work, the more frustrated we become. We put new paint on old programs and add new programs based on the premise that culture is missing key moral and spiritual elements. Andrew Root, a leading scholar in the field of practical theology, noted: "We tend to assume that we've gotten to where we are because things have been subtracted from our cultural lives."[1] Thus we try to shore up those deficiencies. Certainly there are things that once were, and no longer are, part of society. Prayer in schools and the Ten Commandments in courtrooms come to mind. But for the vast majority of Americans, it's not that something has been removed from culture, leaving what used to be referred to as "a God shaped void" in their lives. Rather, the vast majority of

Americans have embraced an entirely different narrative. They sense no need for a god or an externally imposed moral code beyond themselves.

Contemporary culture is more concerned with experience and relationships. The journey to personal authenticity is valued more highly than excellence. Church is still more concerned with intellectual assent to propositional truth. Church still values excellence in presentation and performance, often over-against authenticity. In some areas, culture may not be all wrong. Paul's personal transformation on the Damascus Road was based not on a new set of propositional truths. Rather it was based on his personal encounter with the person of Christ.

There will, I expect, always be a significant role for carefully considered and articulated arguments. But in the 21st century it might be wise for the church to expend less effort on apologetics and more time helping people encounter the person of Christ. Some of the issue comes back to our understanding of what the church really is. We confuse church with the place, or the programs, or the pastor. In order to effectively be the church in the 21st century, we need to start at the beginning. We need to regain a lost sense of what it means to be the body of Christ.

Before we can successfully understand our role in a culture that has no place for truth, we need to understand the foundational elements of what the New Testament calls "church." There are some incredible works out there that go into much more depth on the nature, mission, and structure of the church. For our purposes here, the next three chapters intentionally provide an overview, as we do with our survey of key cultural issues later in this book. Chapter one presents the church as, ecclesia, the Community of the Gospel, centered on the person of Christ. Chapter two will expand on the notion of the Community of the Gospel with the New Testament's charge for that community to proclaim the Gospel both verbally and behaviorally. Then in chapter three we'll consider the biblical basis for our need to understand the culture we live in, and know what to do in that cultural context.

Chapter One

Founding the Church

More years ago than I'd like to admit, I had the opportunity to visit the Italian city of Pisa. There are a lot of great things to see and do in that town. It occurred to me while our bus approached the town, that a non-negotiable experience would be to have pizza for lunch. As it turned out, the most exciting thing about my Italian pizza eating experience wasn't the pizza. It wasn't even eating pizza in the town of Pisa. The truly memorable part of eating pizza in the town of Pisa was that we were eating that pizza in the shadow of the Leaning Tower of Pisa.

The tower is famous, of course, for the fact that it's leaning. The building is actually a bell tower that is part of the Pisa Cathedral. There's some controversy about exactly which architect designed it, so no one knows who to blame. Whoever designed it, the building itself is beautiful. It's all white marble with impressive columns and those big Corinthian capitals. The first floor was built in the mid 1770's. By 1778 work had begun on the second floor and then things started to go wrong. It turns out that the soil is too soft to bear the weight of the building, and the foundation is only ten feet deep. Before work went much further, Pisa went to war with its neighbors and construction stopped.

Almost 100 years later work resumed. The new architect tried to compensate for the tilt and the tower is actually curved. Still, the slow tilt continued until just a few years ago when engineers removed the dirt from under the taller side and declared that the tilting had finally stopped.

It was a lot of fun too, acting like a typical tourist: taking pictures, pretending to hold the tower up. You know the kind of tourist I'm talking about. But it was weird to climb the steps to the top. The tilt made it feel like I was going to fall at any minute. The whole thing felt...wrong.

Hundreds of years after the Leaning Tower of Pisa was constructed, when I was climbing the steps, I wasn't thinking about the architect, or the construction. I was just trying to stand up straight. The step by step battle to the top, and the sense of wrongness, all traced back to the poor foundation.

Just as I wasn't thinking about the poor architectural design, or the type of soil when I was in Pisa, I was also not thinking about what a profound illustration the tower is. Jesus told the story about a foolish man who built his house on the sand. When the storm came, the foundation couldn't hold and the house collapsed. The wise man built his house on a solid foundation that was able to withstand the storm.[2] The principal applies to our twenty-first century church too. As we consider what it means to be God's people in an increasingly chaotic and hostile culture, a good foundation is critical. Without that good foundation our church will be a little like that tower in Pisa: beautiful in concept, but with a slowly increasing tilt that makes everything an uphill battle that just feels wrong.

So we'll start by looking at what the Bible says about the foundation of the church. I don't even try to address every aspect of this topic. Rather, I hope that as you read, God will use this to prompt a deeper understanding and deeper questions about the church in the twenty-first century. As Paul prayed:

I keep asking that the God of our Lord Jesus Christ, the glorious Father, may give you the Spirit of wisdom and revelation, so that you may know him better. I pray that the eyes of your heart may be enlightened in order that you may know the hope to which he has called you, the riches of his glorious inheritance in his holy people, and his incomparably great power for us who believe.[3]

A few years ago I had the incredible opportunity to spend some time in Israel. I've been fortunate in that I've been able to travel to a lot of fascinating places. There's something unique about Israel. Israel is where it all happened. It's the Promised Land from the Old Testament. It's the place where the Messiah was born; the site of his death and resurrection. Israel is where the disciples stopped being fishers of fish, and became fishers of men. Israel is where the church started, which leads us to one of the most amazing places in Israel, to me anyway. It's a town called Caesarea Philippi in the north of the country. The region has a long history of idol worship. Specifically, there's a place just outside town called Panias. At the base of a huge cliff is a cave with a spring of underground water. The area was dedicated to the Greek god Pan who, they believed, was the god of nature and shepherds. As time passed, other religions each added their own stuff. By the time of Christ there was a temple to Caesar, a temple to Zeus and a variety of other, smaller, altars and buildings dedicated to a variety of gods. In addition to the buildings and altars, all over the cliff face, people carved fancy niches for idols.

This physically beautiful, spiritually dark place serves as the backdrop for one of the most significant passages in the Bible. As the story opens, it's around AD 28. Jesus has been traveling around Israel with his disciples for about two and a half years. You probably know a lot of what happened from your own studies, or perhaps from Sunday School when you were young. Israel is occupied by the Romans and they don't like it at all. For generations the Jews have prayed, and they've watched, and they've hoped for the promised Messiah; the one the Old Testament prophets had said would come and save them. The Jews expect this Messiah to restore their national pride, to crush their enemies, to free them from tyranny and oppression. And then Jesus shows up.

Over the course of history lots of different men had shown up claiming to be the Messiah, telling people that it was finally time to rise up and throw off the oppressors. Of course, those revolutions tend to end in crushing defeat. By the first century, some people are desperate enough to believe anything, but most people are just growing skeptical. There is, however, something different about Jesus. He teaches with a kind of authority they've never seen before ... almost like he knows what he's talking about. He does miracles that aren't just illusions: he heals people, he feeds people, he casts out demons, and the crowds are taking note. More and more people are following him around, either waiting to see something exciting, or hoping that maybe, just maybe, God really is doing something amazing this time.

Jesus has already walked on water, calmed the storm, preached the Sermon on the Mount, and even raised a girl from the dead. By the time our story begins, he's decided it would be a good time to take a short retreat with his disciples. They left all the crowds behind and they hiked north until they got to a place called Caesarea Philippi. It's not really clear why he chose that particular place, but I suspect there were a couple of reasons. One was the simple fact that it was away from the big crowds that had become their constant companions. Another reason may have had to do with the history of the place.

As the group approaches the area, the first thing the disciples would have noticed was the setting. They walk along a beautiful, bubbling stream and up to an impressive rock cliff. At the base of the cliff is a beautiful temple covering a huge, dark, foreboding cave opening. As they get a little closer, a multitude of temples and altars come into view. Some are large architectural marvels; others are all but insignificant. Finally, as they walk up to the cliff, they can see hundreds of carved niches, some elaborate, some simple, all dedicated to one false god or another. And all of it centered around that foreboding cave that is said to lead to the underworld.

Matthew chapter 16 tells the story:

> When Jesus came to the region of Caesarea Philippi, he asked his disciples, "Who do people say the Son of Man is?" They replied, "Some say John the Baptist; others say Elijah; and still others, Jeremiah or one of the prophets." "But what about you?" he asked. "Who do you say I am?" Simon Peter answered, "You are the Messiah, the Son of the living God." Jesus replied, "Blessed are you, Simon son of Jonah, for this was not revealed to you by flesh and blood, but by my Father in heaven. And I tell you that you are Peter, and on this rock I will build my church, and the gates of Hades will not overcome it. I will give you the keys of the kingdom of heaven; whatever you bind on earth will be bound in heaven, and whatever you loose on earth will be loosed in heaven." Then he ordered his disciples not to tell anyone that he was the Messiah.[4]

This is one of the most profound and densely packed passages in the Bible. Not surprisingly, it has been hotly debated and discussed for two thousand years. As we look at it from the perspective of church in the twenty-first century, there are three key principles we need to be aware of. First, there's Jesus' statement about building his church on the rock, then an almost passing note about the nature of his church. That's followed quickly by a much more difficult statement about the stewardship of the church.

Building on the Rock

It all begins innocently enough. The disciples are standing there, soaking in the view and trying to make sense of the myriad of temples. Jesus starts with a nice, easy question: "Who do people say I am?" At first blush, there's nothing really scary or intrusive about this. The disciples have been listening to people for months - and everybody has their own theory about Jesus. John the Baptist had been executed not too long before this. Some people think maybe John the Baptist is somehow back from the dead.

Some people think perhaps this is the prophet Ezekiel. Other people wonder if he might be Jeremiah, or maybe another prophet from the Old Testament. Whatever name they give him, almost everyone assumes that Jesus is some kind of forerunner to the Messiah.

All these people are prepared to acknowledge that Jesus is something special; he is from God. But they aren't prepared to acknowledge what's really happening. They've been waiting for the Messiah for hundreds of years, but now that Messiah is finally standing right in front of them, they aren't ready to realize, or admit, it. Think about that for a second: after hundreds of years of praying, waiting, hoping, begging God to send the savior, they are more prepared to think that a dead prophet had come back than to believe that God is really providing the salvation he'd promised.

At this point the conversation is pretty safe with the disciples. "Who do people say I am?" It's just a general conversation about what other people think. And the answers are equally safe and general. "Well, some people think you're Elijah, some people think you're Jeremiah, or maybe John the Baptist. It's kind of flattering really." But then Jesus takes it to the next level. "But who do you say that I am?" The word "you" here is plural; Jesus is asking the whole group what they think.

Can't you just picture an increasingly awkward silence? The twelve disciples are likely shuffling their feet a bit, flicking bits of invisible lint off their shirts, looking up, looking down, looking anywhere but at Jesus. They've been with Jesus long enough to know who he is. They've seen him heal, and teach, and forgive sin, and even raise the dead. Still, no one quite wants to be the first one to answer the question. If you've read much about the disciples, you can guess what happens next. Peter is the one with the big mouth. Peter is the one who jumps without thinking. He's always the first to speak up, even when he doesn't know what he' talking about. In a different discussion, he shot off his mouth and it was so bad Jesus responded with "get behind me Satan!"[5]

It just wasn't in Peter to stay quiet, so while everyone else is trying hard not to be noticed, he blurts out: "You are the Christ, the Son of the living God."[6]

This is probably the most profound statement in the Bible. "Christ" is the Greek word for "Messiah." The Messiah is the Savior, the one talked about in the Old Testament; the one who will make things right between people and God. Standing there in front of that majestic cliff, in front of the beautiful temples to Pan and Caesar and Zeus, Peter is making the bold claim that God is not only a living God, but he's also the source of life. Further, Jesus is that living God. Peter correctly puts all those other notions of god into the position of irrelevance. Peter is brave enough to admit what everyone else is thinking. Jesus isn't just a prophet, or a great teacher, or some kind of amazing spiritual guru. Jesus is the Messiah; God himself; the one who saves people from their broken, fallen, sinful relationship with God. Jesus is the one who will ultimately make all things right.

This time, Jesus didn't correct Peter, or rebuke him, or even just roll his eyes a little. This time Jesus answers him: "Blessed are you Simon Bar-Jonah! For flesh and blood has not revealed this to you, but my Father who is in heaven."[7] "Flesh and blood" was a Jewish way of referring to a human being. We'd be more likely to say "No mere human figured this out Peter. Only God could have given you this kind of insight."

Jesus starts with a relatively simple question: "Who do you say I am?" and once Peter has the guts to admit what they all knew but were afraid to say, Jesus moves on to talk about what's going to come out of that confession. "And I tell you, you are Peter, and on this rock I will build my church ..."[8]

As Jesus talks about rocks and building, imagine how powerful it would have been for the disciples. They're still standing in front of that cliff and the cave and the incredible buildings dedicated to false gods. In this little sentence, in addition to the obvious rocks and buildings metaphors, there's a nuanced little play on the word "rock." The whole book of Matthew was originally written in Greek – the common language at the time. "Peter" in Greek is "petros," which is a masculine word that means "rock." But then Jesus talks about building his church on this rock, and that word he uses is "petra," which is a feminine form of the same word. So what Jesus said was "you are Petros, and on this petra, I will build my church." The word play is subtle enough to create all kinds of different interpretations and keep scholars all worked up.

It's important that we think of this from Peter's vantage point. Peter is obviously being addressed personally here, but there is nothing to indicate that he is more than the mouthpiece of the entire group, so he's not being singled out or placed above the rest of them. Jesus does here acknowledge that Peter has something special going on. He calls Peter "blessed." And in a year or so, Peter really does turn out to be the primary leader of the church. At the same time, it's not about Peter. Jesus doesn't call it "Peter's church;" in a minute Jesus is going to call it "my church."

As important as Peter was, the church is not built on a man. Notice that we're not talking about simple, intellectual assent to a propositional truth. Peter is proclaiming his personal faith in the person of Jesus. The church is built on the person of Jesus the Christ, the Messiah, the son of the living God.

The Community of the Gospel

Standing in the shadow of that imposing rock face, gazing across at the pavilion at the magnificent marble temple exteriors, impressed by the artistry of dozens of niches in the cliff, it would have been logical for the disciples to picture Jesus building a temple to rival that of Solomon. Even as Jesus is talking, they're likely imagining towering pillars, glittering gold trim, deep purple drapes, incense, sacrifices, and all the trappings they've come to associate with the worship of God. Imagine their surprise when Jesus says he's going to build not a building but a people.

The word Jesus uses for "church" is "ecclesia" which has to do with a gathering of people. Jesus' church isn't a building, it's a people. The church is made up of people who make the same claim as Peter did. The church is a people whose faith and lives are centered on the person Jesus as the Christ, the Son of the Living God. Jesus' ecclesia, the church, is to be a Community of the Gospel.

Jesus keeps going: "...on this rock I will build my church, and the gates of hell shall not prevail against it" (Matthew 16:18). The "gates of hell" is a reference to death, and again, Jesus is using word pictures to teach. The huge, deep, dark, cave behind the temple they were standing in front of was thought to be a portal to the underworld and it was sometimes called the gates of hell. In other places the Bible refers to death as the final enemy. If you play video games, you know that every good video game has levels of play that get harder and harder as you go on. If it's one of those 'kill the monster' games, each level has a monster you have to defeat in order to move on to the next level. And of course, each level has a stronger monster. The very last level has the strongest monster of all. Using that analogy, death is that last level – the strongest monster of all. Jesus is saying that not even the power of death, not even the final, most powerful enemy of all, can hope to stand against Jesus' church.

Nothing, not a king, not a president, not a morally bankrupt culture, not even death itself can stand against Jesus' church.

Stewardship of Faith

Jesus maintains that he will build his church. He goes on to say that the church is a people. Next, he introduces something of the role of his church: our responsibility for the stewardship of faith.

> I will give you the keys of the kingdom of heaven; whatever you bind on earth will be bound in heaven, and whatever you loose on earth will be loosed in heaven. Then he ordered his disciples not to tell anyone that he was the Messiah."[9]

If you think the part about Peter being the rock is confusing, try to wrap your brain around what Jesus means with the part about binding and loosing! Once again, scholars are all over the map with their understanding of this statement. We'll leave it to the scholars to argue the fine points of Greek root words. For our purposes it's immensely helpful to realize that the metaphor of keys was not so cryptic in the first century.

Wealthy households of the time typically employed a steward. The steward was a highly trusted servant who was responsible for the well-being of the home. The steward ensured that the lawn was neatly manicured, the fruit trees were watered, the floors were swept, the tapestries were dusted, the meals were excellent, the staff was productive ... you get the idea. The steward was given the literal key to the house, which he would pin on his shoulder. It was a sign of his trusted authority and his heavy responsibility. It was probably also a good way not to lose the key.

The steward was trusted not just to take care of the home, but to do so in a manner that reflected the owner's standards and wishes. It was not the steward's home. He didn't make the standards; he agreed with the owner's standards and ensured the home was run in a manner consistent with them. The steward was given the key as part of his authority and responsibility. With that key, the steward was only given authority to do what was consistent with the home owner's wishes.

As he's talking to the disciples, Christ has given the keys of the kingdom to his church. He has made us his stewards. As stewards we do not make the law, we agree with the law, we obey the law. One Bible translation says it this way:

> I will give you the keys of the kingdom of heaven, and whatever you forbid on earth must be what is

already forbidden in heaven, and whatever you permit on earth must be what is already permitted in heaven.[10]

Jesus is not saying that God will obey whatever we say on earth. Jesus is saying that on earth we must do that which God has already willed. It's also worth noting (again) that Jesus is not limiting his statement to Peter. Peter was just the front man for the rest of the group. Jesus is telling his disciples, his church, that we are to act as stewards for his kingdom. He uses exactly the same terminology when he's speaking to the broader church later in Matthew: "Truly I tell you, whatever you bind on earth will be bound in heaven, and whatever you loose on earth will be loosed in heaven."[11]

As followers of Christ, part of his church, we are stewards. Our authority is limited to what God has already declared in Scripture. Christ places a high level of trust in us. It complements the heavy responsibility we have to steward his church.

So where does that leave us? How do we understand all this so we don't become like that tower in Pisa: beautiful but slowly leaning, slowly falling over through the lack of a strong foundation? As we look at the church in the 21st century, there are three key things we need to take away from Jesus' declaration to his disciples there in Caesarea Philippi. First, the church is built on the person of Christ. Second, the church is a community of faith. And third, the church is responsible to steward that faith. We like to argue the fine points of the first two principles, but we're generally OK with them. It's the third principle that gives us trouble.

Much of the church in America has lost its grasp of the profound reality that we are stewards. Our hearts and intentions are good, but too often we inadvertently create mini kingdoms and then wonder why the world isn't responding the way we want it to. The remainder of this book looks at some of the major issues associated with being the church in the 21st century.

Before we move on though, it makes sense to consider the personal implications of what we've talked about so far.

There's a phrase floating around out there that says "the church is the hope of the world." When you look around that seems kinda lame. Look at how many churches there are, and they all seem to disagree with each other. Churches fight; churches split; churches argue over music and Bible versions and Sunday School curriculum. Each church seems to think that they're the only one who really knows what God wants. How could we possibly say that the church is the hope of the world? The church doesn't have its own act together, what makes us think we can make a difference anywhere else? How can Jesus say that the gates of hell won't prevail? Forget the final enemy…seems like we can destroy our very own selves. But – that is not the kind of thing Jesus is talking about. The church is not the building, or the programs. The church is not about whether my pastor is more eloquent than your pastor, or whether we have a big enough youth group, or whether we give enough money to developing nations. These are all important things, but the church...is people.

When Jesus refers to "my church" he is referring to us. He's referring to his followers, to those who, like Peter, recognize who he is and make the intentional choice to follow him. Acts chapter 2 gives us a quick picture of what church looked like not long after Jesus' death and resurrection:

> And they devoted themselves to the apostles' teaching and the fellowship, to the breaking of bread and the prayers. And awe came upon every soul, and many wonders and signs were being done through the apostles. And all who believed were together and had all things in common. And they were selling their possessions and belongings and distributing the proceeds to all, as any had need. And day by day, attending the temple together and breaking bread in their homes, they received their food with glad and generous hearts, praising God and having favor with all the people. And the Lord added to their number day by day those who were being saved.[12]

Imagine what would happen if we did that. Imagine what would happen if we all devoted ourselves to living our lives based on biblical teaching, and to one another, and to praying for the people around us. Imagine the transformation that would take place in our lives, and then in our city, and our state, and the world. Imagine what would happen if we lived up to the task God has given us as his church.

This is a pretty short passage, but to continue the word play, it provides the bedrock for our understanding of what we're supposed to be about. The whole point of building on bedrock is that it doesn't leave much in the way of wiggle room. This particular bedrock starts with Jesus' personal question: "Who do you say that I am?"

And for those of us who claim Jesus as our Messiah, our Savior, Jesus gives us the awesome responsibility to be his stewards. We don't want to get confused here, Jesus said "I will build my church." He is the one who ultimately builds his people, but we get to play a part. Think about that one: Jesus is going to build his church with us or without us, so in a sense the pressure's off. But would you really want to be left out of something so incredible?

The passage includes a promise: we can place our faith in Jesus, the Christ, the Son of the living God; and he will build his church; and nothing can stand against it. It doesn't matter how scary the Middle East gets, God will continue to draw people to himself. It doesn't matter how complacent we get here in North America, God will continue to draw people to himself. It doesn't matter what's happening in the news today, or tomorrow. Jesus will build his church.

There's some compelling research out there that shows how reflecting on Scripture is the single most effective way to grow spiritually. To reflect on Scripture means to ponder it, to think about it, to consider what it means and how it impacts my life. Take just a moment to consider what the question and the task and the promise actually has to do with you.

Who do you say that Jesus is? Have you come to the point in your life where you're able to say that Jesus is truly the Messiah and that you've put your faith in him? Or are you still undecided? Or do you know he's truly who he says he is, but you haven't really had the guts to make a commitment yet? Jesus asked Peter, one of his more ardent followers, "Who do you say I am?" It wasn't that Jesus didn't already know Peter's heart and mind. Jesus tends to ask questions like that for our reflection. And the question is still the foundational question for Christ-followers today. The church is not, at its heart, an organization. The church is the ecclesia, a people. Before we can truly be the church Jesus intends, we need to ask ourselves the question: "Who do I say he is?"

How are you doing as a steward? Are you faithfully sharing what you know with the people around you? Are you diligently living a life consistent with the wishes of Christ, the one on whose behalf we are stewards?

Jesus will build his church, and nothing, not even the gates of hell itself, can hold it back. What does that promise mean for you? When we look at the state of the world around us, when we consider the state of the church, it's easy to be afraid or to lose hope or to just get angry. The promise is that Jesus' ecclesia will prevail. What was true in the first century is still true in the 21st century: no matter how chaotic our culture gets, no matter how intense persecution becomes, no matter how confused the organized church becomes, the church Jesus builds will prevail.

Chapter Two

Being the Church

I was channel surfing the other day and noticed that you don't have to watch TV very long before you start seeing a whole lot of church channels. There are a whole lot of churches in the world. In the spirit of authenticity: I was not channel surfing to find something meaningful and inspirational. I was looking for something totally brainless that would be a complete waste of my time. But, while I was busy wasting my time, I kept running across different churches. It was fun once I started paying attention. There are massive churches out there with campuses that look like universities, others that meet in full sports stadiums. There are some really different churches out there, including some that beautifully fuse purpose with art and architecture. Others that are built right into rock walls.

Whatever it looks like, almost anywhere we travel, people associate the concept of church with a building. Think about it: as I just described my channel surfing experience, you were very likely picturing similar churches. Or perhaps other churches you've seen in your own travels. Very few people were thinking: "He's not describing church; he's just talking about buildings." When we think of church, we automatically think of buildings, and pastors, and services, and programs.

One of my favorite church experiences ever was in Uganda a couple of years ago. We were visiting a village at what seemed like the ends of the earth; it was really just a couple of hours down a seriously messed up road. There was no building, no programs, no phones, no lights, no motor cars; not a single luxury. That's not really true – we were riding in an SUV, but the theme song to Gilligan's Island seemed to fit. One reason that service ranks so high on my list is that it serves as a powerful reminder. Church isn't about buildings or programs. And as much as it pains my pastor's heart to say it: church isn't about pastors and preaching. The church is people who've chosen to follow Christ. The church is us.

Thirty years after his earth-shattering declaration at Caesarea Philippi, Peter's situation has radically changed. Everything Christ has been preparing him for has come about: Peter's denial of his Messiah, followed by his forgiveness, Christ's death and resurrection, Pentecost and the beginnings of the church. He is not alone, but Peter does indeed become the primary leader of that fledgling church.

It's difficult to be specific about the date, but around AD 64 Peter wrote a letter of encouragement and instruction to the believers in the region we know as modern-day Turkey. The letter, which we know as 1 Peter, is a general letter to all the believers in the entire region rather than to a specific church or town. This was right about the time Nero has begun to persecute Christians as a way to divert attention from his own failure as a leader, and it's apparent throughout the letter that the Christ-followers in the area have begun to experience that persecution.

Peter's instruction has a strong emphasis on how they should live out their faith in an increasingly hostile world.

Matthew introduced us to the fact that Jesus is the foundation of the church. Just a few short years after that profound conversation at Panias, Peter continues that theme in 1 Peter 2. Here's what he says:

> But you are a chosen people, a royal priesthood, a holy nation, God's special possession, that you may declare the praises of him who called you out of darkness into his wonderful light. Once you were not a people, but now you are the people of God; once you had not received mercy, but now you have received mercy. Dear friends, I urge you, as foreigners and exiles, to abstain from sinful desires, which wage war against your soul. Live such good lives among the pagans that, though they accuse you of doing wrong, they may see your good deeds and glorify God on the day he visits us.[13]

As you first read through this, it looks all light and fluffy and happy. We're chosen, we're special, we're the bringers of wonderful light. Those are all good things. But dig a little deeper and it gets a little tougher.

Read the passage again, but before you do, let me point out that this is Peter. He's the same Peter we looked at in the previous chapter. Back in that picturesque setting of Panias, in front of that dark cave, in front of the cliff face full of idols, Peter is the one who has the guts to declare that Jesus is the Christ, the Son of the Living God. Jesus replies "Blessed are you Simon, son of Jonah, because this truth is so deep, so profound, that a mere human could never have figured it out on his own. This truth is so deep, so profound, that only the Most High God could have revealed it to you." And the church, the Community of the Gospel, will be founded on the person of Christ, the Son of the Living God.

Peter reflects here on that foundation, and on what it means to live as Christ's ecclesia, the church:

But you are a chosen people, a royal priesthood, a holy nation, God's special possession, that you may declare the praises of him who called you out of darkness into his wonderful light. Once you were not a people, but now you are the people of God; once you had not received mercy, but now you have received mercy. Dear friends, I urge you, as foreigners and exiles, to abstain from sinful desires, which wage war against your soul. Live such good lives among the pagans that, though they accuse you of doing wrong, they may see your good deeds and glorify God on the day he visits us.

There are three core concepts in this short passage and between them we can understand the heart of what Christ's church is all about.

The first concept is in verse nine where Peter declares that we are "a chosen people." We are ecclesia. Specifically, we are a community centered on the person of Christ; a Community of the Gospel. In that same verse he gives us our second concept: "That you may declare the praises of him who called you out of darkness ..." The

Greek word exangello has to do with the proclamation of the Gospel. Then in verse twelve he says: "live such good lives ... " The third concept is fleshed out by the Greek word anastrophen - the living of the Gospel. Notice how each of these three concepts pulls us to the center, the good news of the person of Christ, the foundation.

Ecclesia: The Community of the Gospel

We looked at this concept a bit in the previous chapter, but we need to spend a little more time on it now. The word "ecclesia" is used throughout the Bible. It has to do with community. This is not a concept that is easy to wrap our 21st century, western brains around. We've been brought up to think in terms of the individual rather than the community. Peter refers to us as "a chosen people, a royal priesthood, a holy nation, God's special possession." We like the idea of being chosen; we like being called royal; holy is a little intimidating, but kinda nice; it's also nice to be special. There's nothing wrong with any of that. How could there be? God put it right there for us to read and celebrate, but it's easy to misunderstand them. Peter pulls each of these four phrases from Old Testament descriptions of God's people.

We too often miss the indefinite article; the letter "a" in front of the word "chosen." That one little letter radically changes the way we should hear Peter. Peter does not say "you are chosen people." He says, "you are a chosen people." We are not a collection of chosen individuals who all get together for church. We are one chosen people. Similarly, Peter does not say "you are royal priests." He says, "you are a royal priesthood." not "holy citizens" but "a holy nation." Not "people belonging to God," but "a people belonging to God." The church, this ecclesia, is a people gathered as a community; a Community of the Gospel; a community based on the fact that our identity is centered on the person of Christ.

A Chosen People

Remember back when you were a kid on the playground and someone was trying to get a football game going? The team captains would take turns picking the best athletes and the most popular kids. As the teams were slowly built, it became readily apparent which kids were wanted and which kids were not wanted. The unwanted kids weren't good at football, or they weren't very popular, or they had something else about them that made each of the teams hope they went to the other team. For some reason they were perceived more as a liability than an asset to the team. The original idea of course was that everyone would get to play and the teams would be fair. In reality it turned into a popularity contest. For a lot of kids it was more about being accepted, or not.

Being part of the Community of the Gospel isn't like that. Ephesians 1:4 says this: "For he chose us in him before the creation of the world to be holy and blameless in his sight. In love he predestined us for the adoption to sonship through Jesus Christ, in accordance with his pleasure and will – ."[14]

We were chosen first. We were chosen before God even created the universe. More than that, God chose a people, a community. He didn't take turns with someone else. He didn't choose us because we were the best and he wanted to win. Nor did he choose us because we were the worst and he felt sorry for us. In a topic for a whole different book sometime, he chose us because he wanted to; it brought him pleasure. And he chose us as a team; a community. We're a chosen people.

A Royal Priesthood

Ironically for a nation that once fought for its independence from a monarchy, America is fascinated with royalty. Not that long ago the news was saturated with accounts of Meghan Markle. Markle, now known as the Duchess of Sussex, was not born into royalty. True, she was a celebrity, but that's just not the same as being a royal. When her engagement to Prince Harry was announced in late 2017, it sparked something in the American psyche. It wasn't quite an aspiration to royalty, but still ... if she could do it, surely someone else could too. And if someone else could become a royal, why couldn't it be me? 11.5 million people tuned in to watch the wedding, making it the third most watched wedding in history. A few weeks later the furor was gone. The news moved on to other, newer things. For that brief moment however, royalty was in reach.

When Peter refers here to Christ-followers as a royal priesthood, he is drawing from God's message to the Israelites where he tells Moses that his people "… will be for me a kingdom of priests."[15] This would have been something of a startling statement for the Jews in both Old and New Testament times. The priesthood is a special honor and responsibility reserved for a single tribe within Israel. It is the priests who served as mediators between God and the people. Only the priests have access to the holy places within the Temple. Similarly, royalty is limited to a specific family within Israel. Only a direct descendent of David can be truly royal. Even within the confines of the Roman empire, the notion of royalty is limited to the emperor and his direct family. Attaining royalty is simply not in the realm of possibility for the Jews. To be both royal and priest is virtually unthinkable. Kings have a specific lineage and set of responsibilities; priests had a completely different lineage and set of responsibilities. With rare exceptions, when kings attempt to fulfill the responsibilities of priests it ends badly. King Uzziah serves as a prime example. 2 Chronicles tells of the time Uzziah's military power, economic strength and personal fame led him to become prideful. In his pride he determined to enter the Temple in order to burn incense, a responsibility reserved for the priests. He was not deterred when priests confronted him and God struck him with leprosy. Uzziah, once a powerful, wealthy, respected king, spent the remainder of his life leprous and exiled from his palace, his people, and the Temple.

Yet Peter insists that we are a royal priesthood. In the context of 1 Peter, the notion includes function (for example, we represent God to the people around us) but the emphasis is on the amazing position that is ours. As ecclesia, we are a royal priesthood with all the rights, privileges and responsibilities pertaining to both the priesthood and the royal family.

We're a chosen people, a royal priesthood, and as if that weren't quite enough, Peter keeps going: we're a holy nation. That's not intimidating.

A Holy Nation

A little earlier in this same letter, Peter wrote: "But just as he who called you is holy, so be holy in all you do; for it is written: 'Be holy, because I am holy.'"[16] Some of us work really hard to be holy. That generally means we try to identify all those things that are bad, and then we try not to do them. It took me a long time to realize that holiness has two sides. In 1 Peter 2, verse 12, Peter tells us to "live such good lives ..." Holiness is not only about avoiding sin, holiness involves the active pursuit of that which is right. We're going to get to that part in a minute. For now, we simply want to keep in mind that as a community we are a holy nation.

Let me take a quick tangent to clarify something. We're instructed to pursue holiness, rightness. Two seconds of self-reflection will confirm for any of us that we're never going to make it. There's no way any of us can actually be perfectly holy. We can only be holy through our relationship with Christ. Notice that he doesn't say we're supposed to become a holy nation. We are supposed to live rightly, but he says we are a holy nation. God has already set us apart. He already looks at his church as holy. As a holy nation, Peter says, we're like foreigners and exiles, and we're called to live out our holy status. We could spend a lot more time on this profound concept, but we're just trying to get an overview, so let's move on.

God's Special Possession

We're God's "special possession." Once again, Peter is pulling from the Old Testament where the prophet Malachi records this: "'On the day when I act,' says the Lord Almighty, 'they will be my treasured possession. I will spare them, just as a father has compassion and spares his son who serves him.'"[17]

The idea here is that we have a special, intimate relationship with God. As a special, or treasured, possession we have the unique privilege of serving him in the context of that intimate relationship. While all of that's true on an individual basis, all the way through Peter's letter, the emphasis is on ecclesia: community. There's something special about the church, about us, together. We are not designed to function in isolation. We're designed to be a community.

Exangello: the Proclamation of the Gospel

After outlining some of what it means to be the Community of the Gospel, Peter urges us to live as strangers and abstain from sinful desires. If you've been in church circles for very long that's nothing new. The bumper sticker version says that we're "in the world but not of the world." The bumper sticker approach isn't too bad when the world around us generally agrees with us. Being a stranger in a place where everyone looks and thinks and talks pretty much the same way isn't hard. But when times change and people do not look like you, or think like you, or talk like you, or even appreciate you, that's when bumper stickers stop working. When the world you're living in starts to push against everything you stand for, it's easier to act like you're part of the crowd. Who wants to be a stranger in a world that hates strangers?

But Peter doesn't slow down to talk about being a stranger. In fact, he barely stops long enough to take a breath before he excitedly moves into his primary point: "that you may declare the praises of him who called you out of darkness and into his wonderful light." In other words, we, this chosen people, this royal priesthood, this holy nation, this special possession, have the immense privilege of pointing people to God. As strangers in the land our focus is to be on our responsibility rather than on our strangeness. The word translated "declare" in this verse is from a Greek word associated with a verbal announcement. In the days before newspapers and social media, kings would send heralds throughout their realm to tell everyone about whatever news the king wanted his people to hear. The herald would generally go to the public square and read the royal edict. That's the kind of thing Peter has in mind here. We're the heralds whose responsibility it is to publicly, verbally proclaim what God has done in and through the Gospel of Christ.

Once again, Peter is drawing from the Old Testament prophets to make his point. Here he references Isaiah where God says: "Forget the former things; do not dwell on the past. See I am doing a new thing! Now it springs up do you not perceive it? ... the people I formed for myself that they may proclaim my praise."[18]

The actual word Peter uses is "exangello" which includes the notion of speaking forth something which is not otherwise known. In other words, if we don't tell people how incredible Jesus is, how are they going to hear?

Anastrophen: the Living of the Gospel

As the passage continues, there's a shift from our position as ecclesia, to a more practical outworking of that intimate relationship and responsibility we have in Christ. He doesn't totally shift gears, however. In verse 12 he says that we should "Live such good lives among the pagans that, though they accuse you of doing wrong, they may see your good deeds and glorify God on the day he visits us."[19]

There's a lot packed into that one little verse, but the part we want to focus on here is that first phrase: "live such good lives." Back in verse nine Peter emphasized our responsibility to declare, to verbally draw attention to the amazing God we serve. Here in verse twelve we learn that we also have a responsibility to live our lives in such a way that we draw attention to that amazing God. The word he uses is "anastrophen." Anastrophen has to do with our behavior, the way we live our lives. We're to live good lives characterized by good deeds.

As a quick side note: when Peter tells us to live good lives among the pagans, "pagans" is not meant as a term of disrespect. To call someone a pagan in the 21st century would either connote intentional adherents of a pagan religion (who, by the way, refer to themselves as pagan), or it would be politically incorrect and likely offensive. It sounds bad to us, but for Peter and his first century readers, a pagan was simply someone who did not identify as a Christian.

Returning to verse 12, the word translated "good" here doesn't just mean "nice." This is not referring to random acts of kindness, or being vaguely polite to the cashier at Walmart. The word is "kalos," and it incorporates both inward and outward lifestyles. It encompasses concepts like moral, ethical, right, honorable, and blameless. "Behavior that is *kalos* is not only good, but also its goodness is apparent and visible to others"[20] Our lives should be so good, so honorable, that even people who don't know Christ will pay attention to him.

Three concepts, three Greek words.

Ecclesia: we are more than a collection of nice people who sit together in nice buildings every weekend. We are a chosen people, a royal priesthood. We are a Community of the Gospel.

Exangello: as that community we are to be heralds of the Gospel. You've probably seen the bumper sticker: "share Christ always, if necessary use words." That's a fun thought, but it's not what the Bible says. We are to verbally proclaim the good news that in Jesus we find light and mercy and belonging.

Anastrophen: as that Community of the Gospel, in addition to our verbal proclamation, we are to live in such a way that people will see what goodness really looks like, and they will recognize Christ.

So now what? If you're young you might get a tattoo with one of those cool new Greek words. For us older folks it'll be fun to find ways to throw three new Greek words into our conversations this week. We'll look spiritual and sound very smart, even if we can't really remember what the words mean. But the point isn't to look spiritual or to sound smart. The point is that our lives will be changed.

It would be relatively easy for most of us to focus on individual life change. As I was working through this passage I kept landing on things I should do. I'm going to live the kind of life that will show others the light of Christ. Or, I'm going to share Christ with someone this week. Those would be good, but they would also miss the point Peter's making. This is a passage about how we, as a community, function. How do I think past myself and think as part of ecclesia? I started to jot down some ideas to conclude this chapter. But the more I worked with what Peter said, the more I felt like everything I came up with was too small, or too limiting, or too specific to my own situation.

Most of us have spent a lot of time in the last couple of years watching the growing moral, emotional, political and spiritual divide in the United States. As a nation, we have some huge issues to deal with: racism, sexism, immigration, ecology, the economy, abuse of power ... the list goes on. As I've paid more and more attention to that stuff, I've found myself getting a little angry with the church, which is kind of ironic since I'm a pastor who does church full time. Why isn't the church doing more? We should be at the forefront of society, not lagging behind the rest of the country. Maybe we should sponsor a dialogue about racial reconciliation. Or create a legal support ministry to help our undocumented friends navigate the immigration maze. Or we could focus some teaching on the abuse of power in relationships. Those are all things that might be good, but as I look at what Peter's telling us, I realize there's something wrong with my assumptions. As a church-going American, my first thought is that the church should do something. But the church is not programs. The church is us. As long as we keep expecting the institution to do something, not much is really going to happen. We have to embrace the responsibility we have as the Community of the Gospel. We need to be proclaiming the Gospel. We need to be living the Gospel. As a community.

For years the church has debated the priority of proclaiming the Gospel versus expressing the social Gospel. Biblically, that makes no sense. They are inextricably linked. Then, as now, the purpose of God's community was, and is, to both proclaim God verbally and behaviorally. The church must fully integrate the proclamation of the Gospel, with a community that reflects the character of Christ, and with lives consistent with the calling to which we are called.

I suggest some ideas in this book, but I certainly don't have all the answers. I don't know specifically what you and your local church should do next. Here's what I do know: doing nothing is not an option. Maintaining the status quo is not an option. Expecting "the church" to do something is not an option.

And once you start imagining what will happen, remember that God intends to do more than we can imagine and he's going to do it in such a way that it draws attention to Christ.

Chapter Three

Understanding the Times

I've considered a lot of different vocations over the course of my life. Right now I'm pretty sure that when I grow up, I want a career as a meteorologist. I realize I'm doing a grave disservice to the complexity of the job, and the integrity most meteorologists bring to it. But really, how great would it be to have a job where no one really expects you to be right most of the time? I'm not currently in a position that requires me to know what's happening outside, and these days I only seem to pay attention to the weather forecast if I'm travelling and need to decide what to pack. Even then, it's just a best guess. Under normal circumstances, it feels best just to look out the window and see whether it looks like rain.

It wasn't all that different back in the first century. Everyone knew that if you wanted to determine what the weather was, you just looked out the window. Jesus uses that common knowledge to point to a more profound truth about understanding what was going on in the world around us. In Matthew 16 we're told that:

> The Pharisees and Sadducees came to Jesus and tested him by asking him to show them a sign from heaven. He replied, "When evening comes, you say, 'It will be fair weather, for the sky is red,' and in the morning, 'Today it will be stormy, for the sky is red and overcast.' You know how to interpret the

appearance of the sky, but you cannot interpret the signs of the times."[21]

It's not that different for most of us. We know how to look out the window to see if it's raining or not, but we don't do that well when it comes to understanding the times we live in. The implication from the passage though, is that we should be able to interpret the signs of the times. Like the Jewish leaders in Jesus' time, we don't seem to do it.

I think there are a couple of reasons for that. Sometimes we're afraid of what might be out there. I read a story not too long ago about a reporter who was interviewing a man who'd just turned 100 years old. Hoping to get a powerful, personal-interest story, the reporter said: "Sir, you must have seen a lot of changes over all those years." "Yup," the man replied. "And I've opposed every one of them." I have no idea if the story is true, but it makes a good point: change is hard and often unwelcome. And it seems like the more change we experience, the harder it gets. So maybe if we don't look out the window we won't have to deal with it.

Another reason we don't do so well when it comes to understanding the times is because we don't know what to look for. The weather's easy. If it's overcast and windy it's time to grab an umbrella. Understanding the world isn't so simple. And most of us just don't look out the window. Unfortunately, as happened with the centenarian, change happens whether we want it to or not. Change happens whether we pay attention or not. It'd be nice if God would just send some clear sign so we couldn't miss it. That's kind of what the Jewish leaders were hoping for: some clear indication of what God was doing and what he expected his people to do. But God doesn't normally work that way. He expects us to read the times a bit like we read the weather: look outside, figure out what's happening, and respond appropriately.

There are all kinds of biblical admonitions to be wise and discerning. There are lots of examples of godly men and women who did just that. There's one example that stands out. The story is told in 1 Chronicles, chapter 12.

David has been hunted for years. It's complicated. Although God called Samuel to anoint David to be the next king of Israel, Saul is still sitting on the throne. Saul, already a deeply troubled man, has become increasingly jealous and paranoid as time passes. Saul and his men chase David until finally David is forced to take refuge with the Philistines – one of Israel's most hated enemies.

Not surprisingly, David has to work hard to win the trust of the Philistines, who are very well aware of who David is. He eventually wins the trust of King Achish who gives him the town of Ziklag. David settles there with his growing army of loyal Israelites. Under King Achish, David is supposed to be attacking the enemies of the Philistines. Unbeknownst to the king, David's agenda is somewhat different. He and his growing army raid the enemies of Israel, protecting the Israelite towns along Israel's southern border. He regularly brings tribute back to Achish further earning the trust of the Philistine king.

While David is doing his thing in Ziklag, the war between Israel and the Philistines continues. Finally, around 1,000 BC the Philistines marshal their armies with the intent of crushing King Saul and the Israelites once and for all. Wisely perhaps, they are afraid that David might decide to support Israel in the coming battle and refuse to have him join the fight. The Philistines absolutely destroy Saul's army. Rather than be captured, Saul commits suicide. And then things get even more confusing for Israel. Everyone knows about David. He is the anointed king of Israel. It would be logical for the nation to rally to him now that Saul is dead. But no, Saul's son Ishbosheth claims the throne and most of the nation follows him. Seven brutal years follow as tribe warred against tribe. Ultimately David overcomes the opposition, at which point we're told that:

> All Israel came together to David at Hebron and said, "We are your own flesh and blood. In the past, even while Saul was king, you were the one who led Israel on their military campaigns. And the Lord your God said to you, 'You will shepherd my people Israel, and you will become their ruler.'" When all the elders of Israel had come to King David at Hebron, he made a covenant with them at Hebron before the Lord, and they anointed David king over Israel, as the Lord had promised through Samuel.[22]

Chapter 12 continues the story by listing the thousands of warriors from the twelve tribes that rally to their new king:

These are the numbers of the men armed for battle
who came to David at Hebron to turn Saul's
kingdom over to him, as the Lord had said:
from Judah, carrying shield and spear—6,800 armed
for battle;
from Simeon, warriors ready for battle—7,100;
from Levi—4,600, including Jehoiada, leader of the
family of Aaron, with 3,700 men, and
Zadok, a brave young warrior, with 22 officers from
his family;
from Benjamin, Saul's tribe—3,000, most of whom
had remained loyal to Saul's house
until then;
from Ephraim, brave warriors, famous in their own
clans—20,800;
from half the tribe of Manasseh, designated by name
to come and make David king—18,000;
from Issachar, men who understood the times and
knew what Israel should do—200 chiefs, with all
their relatives under their command;
from Zebulun, experienced soldiers prepared for
battle with every type of weapon, to help David
with undivided loyalty—50,000;
from Naphtali—1,000 officers, together with 37,000
men carrying shields and spears;
from Dan, ready for battle—28,600;
from Asher, experienced soldiers prepared for
battle—40,000;
and from east of the Jordan, from Reuben, Gad and
the half-tribe of Manasseh, armed with every type
of weapon—120,000.
All these were fighting men who volunteered to serve
in the ranks. They came to Hebron fully

determined to make David king over all Israel. All the rest of the Israelites were also of one mind to make David king.[23]

Israel has been at war with itself and with its enemies for years. The descriptions of the men who show up are understandably militaristic: "carrying shield and spear," "warriors ready for battle, "brave warriors," "experienced soldiers," "armed with every type of weapon." Tucked right in the middle of all those warriors are the men of Issachar. In context these are clearly fighting men just like all the rest, but the description is unique. Rather than being identified as mighty warriors ready for battle, the text says that these are "men who understood the times and knew what Israel should do."

In hindsight, understanding the times seems fairly straightforward. Under God's direction Samuel has anointed David as king over Israel. Israel is in a shooting war with the Philistines. The only logical way to go is to unite under David. Not only is he God's man, he also has a long track record of leading effectively in war.

At the time it would not have been so clear. Saul had been king for many years, but as king he was not following God. Religious confusion was compounded by political confusion. David has been declared a traitor. Further muddying the waters, David has spent the past several years with the Philistines. If they'd had Facebook or Snapchat back then you can imagine the angry nature of the posts. "David's a traitor!" "No, Saul's the traitor." "David is fighting for Israel." No, David is fighting for the Philistines." Even after Saul's death things aren't simple.

His son Ishbosheth claims the throne (which would have been normal practice for royalty in those days) and most of the nation follow him.

It's a confusing, frightening time. Israel's very survival is at stake. The men of Issachar understand the times and know what Israel should do. It's intriguing to consider what makes these few men stand out. How do they seem to understand the times any better than everyone else? How do they know what to do? Unfortunately, we're not told. So we need to go outside this passage to see what else the Bible says about understanding.

The Greek word used for "understanding" here is "sunesis." It's used only a few times in Scripture and it has to do with critical insight. In fairness to Greek and Hebrew scholars, it's worth noting that the 1 Corinthians passage was written in Hebrew. Sunesis is the term used in later Greek translations. I'm defaulting to the Greek here for consistency with the New Testament passages we're about to look at.

Luke uses sunesis when he tells of the time Jesus met with the Temple leaders: "Everyone who heard him was amazed at his understanding [sunesis] and his answers."[24]

Later one of the Jewish leaders uses it when he spoke with Jesus about the greatest commandment: "Well said, teacher," the man replied. "You are right in saying that God is one and there is no other but him. To love him with all your heart, with all your understanding [sunesis] and with all your strength, and to love your neighbor as yourself is more important than all burnt offerings and sacrifices."[25] Jesus, by the way, notes that this is a wise answer.

Later still Paul uses the same term in his letter to the Colossians: "For this reason, since the day we heard about you, we have not stopped praying for you. We continually ask God to fill you with the knowledge of his will through all the wisdom and understanding [sunesis] that the Spirit gives."[26]

You get the idea. When the men of Issachar understand the times, it isn't a superficial awareness of the top news stories of the day. They have a critical insight into what is going on. It's the same kind of understanding we are to have in our relationship with Christ. It's the same kind of understanding Paul prays the Colossians will gain.

Which brings us back to Jesus' analogy of the weather. For those Jewish leaders to have understood the weather took at least some intentionality. In order to understand the weather, we have to pay attention to the sky. We have to look at what it's doing, feel the wind, sense the temperature. Then we have to think about it; we have to put all the pieces together and consider what it means.

The men of Issachar don't stop to pat themselves on the back for their deep understanding of the times. They take the next step and figure out what Israel should do. Once we put all the pieces together, we need to figure out what we should do, then act appropriately.

Weather is easy, at least the part about looking out the window to see if we need to grab an umbrella. Most of the time we don't even realize how much information we're processing when we look out that window. Culture, now that's hard. I'm convinced that's why the men of Issachar stand out. All the warriors understand the weather. Understanding the times is altogether different, and it is apparently just these 200 leaders from Issachar who have put all the pieces together. Understanding the times takes intentionality. We have to pay attention to what is changing. We have to look at what culture is doing. We have to feel which way the winds of culture are blowing. We have to sense the cultural temperature. Then we have to think about it. We have to overlay what we're now aware of with what we know about culture. We also have to run that through a biblical world view. That's a lot of effort many people aren't willing to give. And so we don't often understand the times or know what the church should do.

Then men of Issachar understand the times. Keep in mind that these are not scholars in ivory towers writing theoretical treatises on contemporary culture. These 200 men are leaders. They have real life responsibilities. They have jobs and families. Even so, not only do they understand the signs of the times, they also know the best course for Israel to take. They paid attention to what was going on in the world around them. They figured out how best to respond. As important as it is for us to be knowledgeable and discerning about what's going on in our culture, understanding the times isn't enough on its own. We have to know what to do about it, and then do it.

Many years before King David, Joshua led God's people into the Promised Land. Those people had seen God do incredible things as they crossed the Jordan River, watched the walls of Jericho fall, and ultimately took possession of the land. We're told that they "...served the Lord throughout the lifetime of Joshua and of the elders who outlived him and who had seen the great things the Lord had done for Israel."[27] Inevitably, the elders followed Joshua in death. "After that whole generation had been gathered to their ancestors, another generation grew up who knew neither the Lord nor what he had done for Israel. Then the Israelites did evil in the eyes of the Lord and served the Baals."[28] It took only a single generation for people to lose their understanding. One single generation for the nation of Israel to stop worshipping God and start worshipping Baal.

As we look at the nation we live in; as we study the trends in faith and church, it feels like we're not too far from a similar catastrophe. The world around us has shifted. Many in the church have applied a biblical world view to culture and found it to be a harsh rain. But then rather than considering a biblical response to that shifting world, many have simply slammed the window shut in a vain attempt to keep the rain out. As a pastor and consultant, I'm concerned that the church in American has not, and is not, shifting with culture. I'm not suggesting that God has changed, or that his word has changed. Nor am I suggesting that the foundational, biblical elements of the church have or should have somehow changed. I am suggesting, however, that the way to go about doing church needs to change. If we're going to effectively live as the Community of the Gospel, we need to find ways of doing and being church that make sense in the new culture we find ourselves in.

Mark Twain is said to have opined that the only person who likes change is a wet baby. Let's face it: we don't want to change. We like the way things are, or were. The way we do things now is the way we've always done things. The way we do things now worked for us. Our programs, our systems and our assumptions changed our lives. We came to know Christ and grew in our faith through those things. The way we worship is profoundly meaningful to us. The way we design our buildings is comfortable to us. The way we approach evangelism makes sense to us. To us. But it's not about us. Research tells us that people are not being attracted to Christ, let alone to our churches. Culture is growing further from God, not closer.

As we work to understand the times, and as we work to know what to do, we have to be willing to take a hard look at our biases and assumptions. We then have to filter those assumptions through the lens of Scripture. Part of figuring out what to do includes making sure we can differentiate between those things in our Christian experience that are personal preferences, and those things that are biblical principles. As this book unfolds we're going to spend more time on some of the cultural issues facing the church, which is why we began with a review of what the church really is. We know it in our heads, but it's really hard to remember that our programs and pastors, our systems and our structures, are not the church.

In order to be like the men of Issachar, we need three things. First, we need to be intentional in our pursuit of understanding. We need to read books we don't care for. We need to watch news channels we don't agree with. We need to respectfully interact with people who don't think like us. Second, we need to thoughtfully act on that newfound understanding. That thoughtful action requires us to painstakingly distinguish between personal preferences and biblical principles. That thoughtful action will often require us to sacrifice those personal preferences in order to promote biblical principles in a changing culture. Third, we need unwavering reliance on the Holy Spirit.

In the Old Testament Daniel was a Jew holding a high level position in the Babylonian government. You probably know of the time King Nebuchadnezzar had a dream and demanded that his wise men not only interpret the dream, but tell him what the dream was. When they couldn't do it, Nebuchadnezzar ordered the execution of all his wise men, including Daniel. God revealed both the dream and its meaning to Daniel. The book of Daniel records Daniel's prayer:

During the night the mystery was revealed to Daniel in a vision. Then Daniel praised the God of heaven and said: "Praise be to the name of God for ever and ever; wisdom and power are his. He changes times and seasons; he deposes kings and raises up others. He gives wisdom to the wise and knowledge to the discerning. He reveals deep and hidden things; he knows what lies in darkness, and light dwells with him. I thank and praise you, God of my ancestors: You have given me wisdom and power, you have made known to me what we asked of you, you have made known to us the dream of the king."[29]

Much like Daniel and King Nebuchadnezzar's dream, there is no way we can truly discern everything that's going on around us. Much less will we be able to devise a plan of action. It is God who gives wisdom and power. It is God who makes known to us what we ask of him.

Now comes the hard part. It's fun to consider the meaning of biblical words. It's interesting to wonder what those 200 chiefs from Issachar were like. But we do God's word a grave disservice if we treat it like a textbook. David said that God's word is like a light for our paths. It's meant to help us move forward. And it's not always a pleasant proposition because it means work and it means change. But, that's why I wrote and you're reading this. Right? We want to become more of the men and women God wants us to become. We want to become more of the Community of the Gospel we're supposed to be. We want what Paul prayed for the Colossians, that we would be filled "With the knowledge of his will through all the wisdom and understanding [sunesis] that the Spirit gives."[30]

The church desperately needs to be like the men of Issachar. Some of us have formal leadership roles we can leverage within the context of our local churches. Most of us don't have formal leadership roles. Keep in mind what we've seen regarding the nature of the church. The church is not the pastors and programs. It's not the systems and structures. The church is us. Together. We need to be men and women who understand the times and know what the church should do.

Section Two

Political strategist Doug Soznick is convinced that American is "going through the most significant period of change since the beginning of the Industrial Revolution."[31] Journalist Kyle Smith laments that "We've hardly taken notice of it, because it happened in people's minds instead of in the streets, happened in ordinary people instead of in the elites and the punditocracy. Compared to just a few years ago, we have a completely different set of ideas about what constitutes acceptable behavior.[32]" From our behavior to our values to our thought patterns, it's obvious that American has undergone a phenomenal cultural shift.

With cultural norms deeply embedded in the American church, the church is going through much the same massive upheaval. Phyllis Tickle, renowned religious historian, reminds us that "...every five hundred years the empowered structures of institutionalized Christianity, whatever they may be at that time, become an intolerable carapace that must be shattered in order that renewal and new growth may occur."[33] We are, she states, in one such time. Jenkins, another expert in religion, begins his study of the what he dubs "the next Christendom" in agreement with Tickle: "We are currently living through one of the transforming moments in the history of religion worldwide."[34]

The shift has been decades in the making yet it is, in the words of Tickle "...amorphous, lacking any cohesion or, for that matter, any clear borders of definable circumference."[35] Despite the titanic nature of this shift, it caught most of us unaware and we're still unsure of its cohesion or where the borders lie. Difficult as the task may be, Tickle, Jenkins, Soznick and many others draw our attention to the need to understand the culture and time we live in.

There are limitless possibilities when it comes to methods by which we can begin to grasp what's happening around us. There is a dizzying array of potential issues to investigate, multitudes of studies to assimilate and hundreds of anecdotes to consider. Knowing well that I do injustice to many key elements and nuances, I see nine core trends the church in America needs to be aware of. They group roughly into three areas, each of which we'll survey briefly in this section. The first is a paradigm shift, a fundamental change in the way people look at the world around them. Chapter four looks at the way the locus of Christianity has moved from the West to the Global South; a move with tremendous implications for the understanding of Christian theology as well as the practice of church. The chapter then considers the nature and impact of secularization in American, followed by a discussion of centered-set thinking. Chapter five moves on to the shift in culture as generation replaces generation. In addition to the chronological generations, this chapter considers the impact of electronics on the way people think and act. It concludes with a brief discussion of key values as generations and culture changes. Finally, chapter six looks at the issue of justice as perhaps the single most pressing priority of this new culture. The chapter breaks this priority into concerns of social, individual and environmental justice.

In each of these chapters I attempt to describe the cultural reality we now live in, identify some of the implications for Christ's church, and surround the discussion with a biblical worldview. None of the chapters can possibly do justice to any of the issues. Rather, they are intended to raise awareness and understanding, so we are in a better position to know what the church should do.

Chapter Four

Paradigm Shift

Global South

There I was, sitting in one of my favorite coffee haunts, dark roast in hand, chatting with Dr. Phillip Wandawa. Phillip is a pastor, theologian, and Principal at Kampala Evangelical School of Theology. I'd visited KEST a couple of years previously as my church was exploring the possibility of a partnership in Uganda. We didn't have anything particular in mind, but we knew we wanted something more than a traditional "we'll send you money and call it a partnership." We were looking for a relational as well as financial investment; and we believed that partnerships go both ways. Phillip hadn't been in Uganda at the time, so this was my first opportunity to discuss with him what a partnership might look like.

We spoke briefly of ways my church could support KEST, and then I asked Phillip how he thought my church might benefit from the partnership. This wasn't a question of us getting some kind of return-on-investment. We were looking for a true partnership where both sides grew. I wanted to know what he might be able to teach us. There was a brief moment of silence, after which I got the impression that Philip had rarely been asked that question before. Embarrassingly, American churches and leaders had always assumed they had not only the financial resources, but the knowledge and spiritual maturity. It had not occurred to them that we can learn as much from the Ugandan church as the Ugandan church can learn from us.

Phillip knows his stuff. He has some deep insight regarding the history and growth of the church in Africa. Our hour together went all too quickly as he taught me about African spirituality and culture. I was struck by the fact that Christianity is not only thriving in Africa, but African theologians like Dr. Wandawa are bringing their own experience, culture and wisdom to bear. And it's not just happening in Africa. While Christianity appears to be on the wane in the United States (we'll consider that later), that cannot be said for Christianity as a whole.

In 2013 The Center for the Study of Global Christianity, out of Gordon-Conwell Theological Seminary, published a comprehensive report on world Christianity. They noted a "... great shift of Christianity to the global South ..." toward the end of the twentieth century and predicted that the "... trend would continue into the future." According to their research, in 1970 40 percent of Christians lived in Europe and 17 percent lived in North America. At the same time, 11 percent lived in Africa. The numbers have dramatically shifted in the past several decades. "Due to the continued growth of Christianity in Africa, the share of all Christians living on that continent is expected to rise to 24.7% by 2020, ... Northern America, meanwhile, has seen its share fall from 17.2% in 1970 to 12.0% in 2010 (and an expected 11.3% by 2020)."[36] In 2018 66 percent of Christians live in the global South.[37]

There are, of course, many different ways to categorize people within the sociologically broad rubric of "Christian." The World Christian Database (a primary source for The Center for the Study of Global Christianity referenced above) casts the widest net, including every group which claims to follow Christ (Anglicans, Catholics, Protestants, Mormons and others). That same database, along with others such as Operation World, also looks more specifically at the more narrowly defined Evangelical Christianity. These major data sources vary in their estimates, but whether viewed through a broad or a narrow rubric, all agree that there are more Christians in Africa (and Asia) than in America. They also agree that the gap is widening.

Clearly the center of gravity for Christianity is moving from the west to the south. Even within the geographic confines of the United States the paradigm is shifting as the church moves away from its historically Anglo foundation. A recent Pew study reported that even as mainline Protestant church attendance dropped from 41 million in 2007 to 36 million in 2014, the percentage of non-whites in those churches rose from nine to 14 percent.[38] Evangelical Protestant churches saw a similar increase, with non-Anglos growing from 19 percent in 2007 to almost 25% in 2014. This trend is amplified in younger generations: "Among all those in the United States who are sixty-five or older today, nearly two-thirds are either white Protestants, white Catholics, or white evangelicals. But among those who are eighteen to twenty-one, white believers make up only 28 percent of that total group."[39] Philip Jenkins makes the compelling case that by 2050 only one in five Christians will be

Anglo.[40] For the countless thousands of Western missionaries and churches who poured their lives and resources into the church in Africa, Asia, and Latin America, it's exhilarating to see the fruit of that labor exceed our wildest expectations. At the same time, most of the church in America is completely unprepared for the implications of the shift.

A (stereo)-typical Anglo church in America views the Christian faith through the lens of modern, Western culture. Andrew Walls, author and Christian historian, notes that "The most striking feature of Christianity at the beginning of the third millennium is that it is predominantly a non-Western religion. ... We have long been used to a Christian theology that was shaped by the interaction of Christian faith with Greek philosophy and Roman law. ... These forms have become so familiar and established that we have come to think of them as normal and characteristic forms of Christianity."[41] We approach life and faith from the perspective of individual over-against community. And we focus on the rational, material world we can see, touch, control and explain. There's more, of course, but those two themes summarize much of our Anglo paradigm. That paradigm is rapidly losing ground as the locus of Christianity moves away from the western world.

The paradigm shift is quickened by the reality that international missionaries from the global South are increasing, while missionary sending from the North is decreasing. In 2010 the United States sent the most missionaries to other countries (127,000) but ranked only ninth in the number of missionaries sent per capita (the U.S. sent 614 international missionaries per million church members). Among those ranked higher than the U.S. were Singapore (815 missionaries per million church members) and South Korea (1,014). Palestine ranked first, sending 3,401 missionaries per million church members. Many of the missionaries from the global South are serving in the North. Interestingly, the U.S. received the highest number of international missionaries of any single nation (32,400).[42]

Many, though certainly not all, of these missionaries are sent by national churches to those living in diaspora. The Pew Research Center estimated that in 2017 almost 50 million people currently living in America were born in other countries.[43] Other studies have estimated that approximately half of all global immigrants are Christians.[44] If those estimates are even close to correct, there are 25 million Christians living in the United States who were born in other countries.

As Christianity moves from western culture into the non-western world, the way we view the interaction of faith and culture, including our approach to "doing church," is being challenged. As non-western thought, culture and underlying assumptions increasingly challenge a purely Anglo understanding of our faith, it becomes important that we embrace the learning process. Wesley Granberg-Michaelson bluntly notes: "The truth is that the glasses of the Western Enlightenment that have framed our view of the world now obscure reality more than reveal it."[45]

The church needs to recognize that for better or worse people bring their native culture, including faith, with

67

them. "Not only does the faith of the migrants internally change, but their communities, with their rich traditions and deep-seated beliefs, also significantly alter the religious landscapes of the countries in which they settle. ... Changing religious landscapes affects local politics, cultures, and societies in significant ways, and studying the religious affiliations of migrants will enable communities to make the necessary changes and offer vital support for migrants and non-migrants alike."[46]

The overwhelming majority of Christian scholarship and writing in areas such as theology, ecclesiology, and missiology is based on the cultural assumptions of western, Anglo, older men. That appears to be changing in many of our churches, Christian universities, and seminaries, but the change is slow to come. The trickledown effect to pastors and other church leaders is even slower. Meanwhile, as the global church shifts to the south, other voices are rising above the noise. The American church desperately needs to seek out and learn from those voices. Most of us are so steeped in our own cultural norms that the writing of other cultures feels uncomfortable at best. We must pursue not only the more academic writings readily available, but we must also pursue open dialogue with people from other cultures and other ways of approaching their relationship with Christ. We need to put on humility, put aside our defensiveness, and be open to the amazing ways our corporate and individual faith can be deepened by new ways of thinking.

Secularization

Early in 2016 the Washington Post published an article in which it declared the end of "Christian America."[47] The author argued that America can no longer be called a Christian nation because it no longer attempts to live out a Christian faith. Two years later, in a similar article, the Christian Broadcast Network ran an article called "The First Post-Christian Generation?"[48] The article noted that 35% of Generation Z (those born between 1996 and 2010, and affectionately known as GenZ) is atheist, agnostic, or at best, unaffiliated with any faith.

Tom Gilson, Christian author and editor of The Stream, takes the "post-Christian" concept a step farther, suggesting that we're far past "post-Christian" and need to stop defining ourselves by what we used to be. "A new faith has swept the old one totally aside. It is a faith of new gods ... *we ourselves* are the gods. ... Self-worship in the past has always been tempered by belief in some other, higher gods who set the rules, defined good and evil, punished evildoers, and determined the way their worshipers could attain the ultimate good, whatever that might be. ... This new religion's creed is summed up in the belief that each person should attain maximum godhood without hindrance."[49]

Albert Mohler asserts that "The story of the rise of secularism is a stunning intellectual and moral revolution. It defies exaggeration. We must recognize that it is far more pervasive than we might want to believe, for this intellectual revolution has changed the worldviews of even those who *believe* themselves to be opposed to it."[50]

For some of us, the idea that America has become a secular society comes as something of a surprise. We knew things aren't great, but assumed the foundational elements of America as a Christian nation remained intact. Gilson's article was one of many responses to a report published by Barna Group in 2016. The report was far-reaching, covering everything from employment to politics and from sexuality to social media. Of particular note were the findings related to faith and church.

In general, trends are not encouraging. Over the past thirty years, church attendance has ebbed and flowed, but where in 1986 48% of Americans reported attending church in the past week, that number had dropped to 35% in 2016. An additional 44% reported not attending church at all in the previous six months. The numbers are even more dramatic when broken down by generation. 48% of Elders (those born before 1946) had been to church in the past week. That compares to 35% of Boomers (1946-1964), 33% of Gen Xers (1965-1983), and 28% of Millennials (also called Gen Y) (1984-2002). Looked at from a different perspective, Millennials make up 17% of the population in America but only 10% of the population in churches.[51] Early indicators suggest that Gen Z (1996-2010) are even less likely to attend. One key part of the equation is the growing distrust in institutions, including government, business, and church. Barna notes that "coupled with a broader secularizing trend, this anti-institutional sentiment has caused an overall decline in church attendance among the general population."[52] That anti-institutional sentiment is reflected in low levels of confidence Americans have in religion in general and churches in particular. For example, only 48% of regular church attenders are confident in the church's ability to provide teaching about Jesus; only 42% think the church can instill morals or values.[53]

Secularization is the process in which a society transforms from religious affiliations and values to a different set of nonreligious affiliations and values. The more secular a society becomes, the less significance it places on religion. Religious faith loses cultural authority and religious organizations lose institutional power. Eventually that society begins to embrace secularism, which is an ideology identified, in part, by the conspicuous absence of a binding authority or belief in God. As society becomes increasingly secular, there is a corresponding increase in the rejection of religion and its values. In America "this means that the church is losing its influence as a shaper of life and thought in the wider social order, and Christianity is losing its place as the dominant world view."[54] Certainly this secularization did not begin suddenly and in a vacuum. Some scholars suggest that it started in the eighteenth century with the Enlightenment and the rise of science. Others maintain that it all began in the 1960's with the assassination of President Kennedy, the civil rights struggle, and the hippie movement. Still others claim that Watergate was the pivotal event the caused the erosion of faith in God and government. Whatever the historical genesis, research is clear that secularism has largely replaced religion in the psyche of the American culture.

Peter Berger, known for his work in the sociology of religion, argues that in the twentieth century Christianity morphed into something optional and noncognitive; in other words, people do not feel the need to make a conscious choice to believe. "As a result, the binding authority of the Christian moral tradition or of any religious tradition was lost. Consequently, many of our friends and neighbors continued to profess faith in God, but that profession was ultimately devoid of any moral authority or cognitive context."[55]

As Christianity, for many, left behind cognitive commitments and an awareness of binding authority, secularism asserted a more compelling pull on their worldview. Thus we see that as little as a decade ago, the majority of the American population opposed same-sex marriage. Recent polls have shown a distinct change of heart, with the majority now favoring the very thing they opposed a few short years ago."... When the cultural tide turned against our society's empty religious commitments, people where happy to jettison their moral judgment ... to retain their social capital."[56]

Secularization does not necessarily equate to a lack of religiosity. On the contrary, many people consider themselves to be spiritual. However, belief in anything, or in any combination of things, is considered an optional, distinctly personal, choice. Though spirituality and some form of religiosity are in vogue, twenty-first century spirituality rejects belief in the personal, authoritative God of traditional Christianity.

When most of us think of America becoming more secular, we tend to think of things like prayer in schools, Ten Commandments in courtrooms and the Freedom From Religion Foundation that seems to be everywhere. We think that if we could just get prayer back in the schools and the Ten Commandments back in the courtrooms, life would get back to the way it should be. Unfortunately, those are just the sideshows. The real issue with secularism is much more profound.

As secularization takes hold in America, people are pulled more and more strongly toward secularism and away from Christianity. A generation ago people tended to identify with Christianity and go to church, in part because culture pulled them in that direction. Think of it as a bell curve. Not that many years ago, the cultural bell curve favored the church. Some people were on the far end, totally committed to Christ and his church. Others were all the way on the other side, totally rejecting anything to do with God. Most people were somewhere in the middle, more influenced by culture than by any strong personal commitment. When you asked someone about religion they'd generally say they were Christian because that was the appropriate thing to say. Most people affiliated with a church because that was the culturally appropriate thing to do. This tendency created the heart of the church's American mission field. Those were the people that prompted the church's movement to attract and reach "seekers." They were open, cautious but curious, and would look to the church for answers and solace. It was also this group of seekers who formed a natural connection between the church and the non-churched world.

The bell curve has shifted and that connection is all but gone. In our increasingly secular culture "if asked about religion, people in the center say they're nothing, because that's the cultural thing to say. And they don't go to church because that is the cultural thing *not* to do."[57] That shifting bell curve presents a huge challenge to our assumptions about people being open to church. They're simply not interested any more, and in the absence of specific interest, they're looking elsewhere for answers and meaning.

There's a related phenomenon in our young people that's been dubbed "the rise of the nones." Conventional wisdom has long held that young people will, almost as a rite of passage, leave their churches behind as they head off to college. A few years later, these young people settle down with families, jobs and all the responsibilities associated with adulthood. At which point, they inevitably meander back to their roots in church.

In 2008 the American Religious Identification Survey showed a startling statistic. 15% of Americans selected "none" for their religious preference, almost twice as many as in a similar study eighteen years previously.[58] Other studies, including the National Study of Youth and Religion, have shown the same thing. The Pew Forum on Religion and Public Life found that by 2012 the number had increased to over 19%. A new generation of Americans has bucked conventional wisdom; this next generation has not returned to church as expected. Among young adults, a staggering 40% were indifferent or irreligious, compared with only 15% who were committed to their faith. In the 1940's only 5% of the population was unaffiliated with religion. James White, author of "The Rise of the Nones," notes that "The nones now make up the nation's fastest-growing and second-largest religious category, eclipsed only by Catholics, outnumbering even Southern Baptists, the largest Protestant denomination."[59] The spiritual, social, ethical, and moral implications of this shift can hardly be underestimated.

Disturbingly, at least for concerned Christians, it's not that the next generation is open to God but not to institutionalized religion. And it's not that they're rejecting God, or even church. They simply don't care. They tend to consider themselves spiritual, and at least open to the possibility that there's a God, but they're not pursuing God or religion. I was having lunch in my favorite pizza place not too long ago. The pizza is great, it's not that expensive, and they'll make it exactly the way I want it. As I looked around at others enjoying their pizza, I realized that as much as I like this pizza place, someone who isn't interested in pizza won't care. It's not that they have something against pizza, but they're not going to stop there for lunch. They'll readily acknowledge that some people like pizza, but again, it simply doesn't matter to them.

For those of us who grew up in a culture that valued, or at least acknowledged value in, God, faith and the church, it's really hard to wrap our brains around the fact that the church no longer holds the place it used to hold. Fewer and fewer people are attending church in America and we can expect that trend to continue. It will likely accelerate as older generations give way to younger. With the bell curve moving away from church, traditional forms of evangelism and church growth programs are less and less effective. Traditional programs and classes designed to educate and disciple are similarly decreasing in effectiveness. Volunteerism in church no longer sustains systems and structures that once flourished.

This is not the first time God's people have found themselves living in a society that is not interested in God. In 605 BC the Babylonians took a young man named Daniel, and a whole lot of other royalty, from the nation of Judah and determined to turn them into good Babylonian officials. Daniel was probably about 15 at the time. Daniel chapter 1 records the story:

> In the third year of the reign of Jehoiakim king of Judah, Nebuchadnezzar king of Babylon came to Jerusalem and besieged it. And the Lord delivered Jehoiakim king of Judah into his hand, along with some of the articles from the temple of God. These he carried off to the temple of his god in Babylonia and put in the treasure house of his god. Then the king ordered Ashpenaz, chief of his court officials, to bring into the king's service some of the Israelites from the royal family and the nobility— young men without any physical defect, handsome, showing aptitude for every kind of learning, well informed, quick to understand, and qualified to serve in the king's palace. He was to teach them the language and

literature of the Babylonians. The king assigned them a daily amount of food and wine from the king's table. They were to be trained for three years, and after that they were to enter the king's service. Among those who were chosen were some from Judah: Daniel, Hananiah, Mishael and Azariah. The chief official gave them new names: to Daniel, the name Belteshazzar; to Hananiah, Shadrach; to Mishael, Meshach; and to Azariah, Abednego. But Daniel resolved not to defile himself with the royal food and wine, and he asked the chief official for permission not to defile himself this way.[60]

Right about the time Daniel was old enough to drive, he was taken from his Jewish home and culture, then thrust into the service of another nation. A nation that worshipped false gods. The Jewish nation had lots of problems, and they continued to struggle with idolatry and disobedience, but it was still Judah and it still retained a fundamental awareness of God. Imagine what it must have felt like for Daniel. Disoriented by the massive cultural shift he was going through. Desperate to follow God in a world that made it more and more difficult to do so. Confused about why the people around him didn't want anything to do with the real God.

Daniel figured out that to honor God he was going to have to be a godly man in a godless culture. As I read through the story of Daniel, I see three things he did that are relevant to us today.

First, he worked hard to understand his new culture. We already saw that Daniel was forced into a crash course in

Babylonian culture. As a prospective Babylonian official, he was required to learn the language and the literature of his new nation. Language and literature would have included the history, philosophy, laws and religion of Babylon.

We know what happened next:

> At the end of the time set by the king to bring them into his service, the chief official presented them to Nebuchadnezzar. The king talked with them, and he found none equal to Daniel, Hananiah, Mishael and Azariah; so they entered the king's service. In every matter of wisdom and understanding about which the king questioned them, he found them ten times better than all the magicians and enchanters in his whole kingdom. And Daniel remained there until the first year of King Cyrus.[61]

None of the others were equal to these Jewish men. This is the kind of understanding shown by the men of Issachar. It was sunesis: a holistic, critical understanding of what was happening in the world around them.

Second, while he immersed himself in his work to understand Babylonian culture, Daniel was diligent in the practice of his own faith in God. Right from the beginning he asked for permission to eat a different diet, one required by his faith. The food from the king's table would have been only the best. It would also have been part of worship and sacrifice to the Babylonian gods; thus it would have been considered unclean by the Jews. We know this wasn't just a burst of youthful zeal or defiance. Daniel continued to practice his faith throughout his life. Many years after he was taken to Babylon, we read this in Daniel chapter six:

> Now when Daniel learned that the decree had been published, he went home to his upstairs room where the windows opened toward Jerusalem. Three times a day he got down on his knees and prayed, giving thanks to his God, just as he had done before.[62]

Even in the face of strong opposition, Daniel prayed three times a day "just as he had done before." In other words, he had been praying like that all along. In Daniel's efforts to be a godly man in a godless culture, he worked hard to understand the culture around him. He was also diligent in the pursuit of his own faith, from his diet to his prayer life. Then, because he did the first two, he was in a position to fully engage in the society he fundamentally disagreed with.

We know Daniel as a brave, godly young man. We almost always forget that he grew up. Notice that last verse in Daniel chapter one: "And Daniel remained there until the first year of King Cyrus." Daniel was about 80 years old in the first year of King Cyrus. He was still providing wise leadership to a godless nation. He was an octogenarian when he was thrown into the lion's den for living out his faith in that culture.

His entire adult life was spent understanding the times and knowing what to do. When he first came to prominence it was precisely because he studied Babylonian culture so well he surpassed even his

Babylonian peers. All the while he faithfully followed God in such a way that others noticed God too.

There are some strong similarities between Daniel in the sixth century BC and us in the 21st century AD. Like Daniel, we find ourselves moving from a culture that had God as a central feature to something completely different. Like Daniel we can find ourselves disoriented by the massive cultural shift; desperate to follow God in a world that seems determined to make that more and more difficult. Sometimes confused about why people don't seem to have any interest in the things of God. Also like Daniel, we must find a way to be godly people in a godless culture.

Centered Set

While I was subjecting myself to the proverbial fire hose of information that's part and parcel of any good class in a doctoral program, one of the influential professors at my school was Dr. Paul Hiebert. Dr. Hiebert was one of the world's leading missiological anthropologists (that is, he studied the complex interactions between missions, culture and people). One of his most profound discussions had to do with the way we categorize the world around us. Specifically, he spoke of the fundamental difference between "bounded set" and "centered set" thinking. A relatively simple example is found in the difference between an Old Testament Hebrew and New Testament Greek world view. The Hebrews thought of things in terms of their extrinsic relationship to others. God, for example, was spoken of as the God of Abraham, Isaac, and Jacob. Greek thought emphasized things in terms of their intrinsic attributes: God is omniscient and omnipotent regardless of his relationship with others. To oversimplify, traditional, Western, Anglo thinking tends to revolve around bounded sets, while most of the rest of the world, and much of the younger Anglo generation, thinks in terms of centered sets. With this in mind, most Western church teaching is based on bounded set thinking. We teach that God is best understood by his own personal character and attributes. Most non-western cultures would best understand God by looking at his relationship with us and with his creation.

With bounded set thinking, the emphasis is logically on the boundary itself. Whatever thing, or person, we're considering is either inside, or it is outside, the set as defined by the boundary. "Bounded-set cultures develop taxonomies and logical systems and categories for everything."[63] We develop a clear definition (boundary) for fruit; which dictates that the thing we hold in our hand is either a fruit or it is not a fruit; it cannot be both a fruit and not a fruit. Even within the bounded set of fruit, we categorize: an apple cannot be an orange. We do the same thing with people that we do with plants (a person is a Christian or not a Christian, a member or not a member). And we do the same thing with theology (the entire basis for "systematic theology" is bounded set thinking). Hiebert notes that salvation is viewed as a "single dramatic crossing of the boundary between being a non-Christian and being Christian. We would expect all believers to enter by the same door, share the same basic theological doctrines, and behave in the same basic way."[64] Any other experience of conversion is suspect, at best.

As deeply ingrained as bounded set thinking is within American culture, and hence the American church, boundaries and bounded set thinking is quietly shifting, particularly in the younger generations. They simply don't think the way we older folks do. I was in a conversation with a young pastor friend of mine when the conversation turned to the topic of salvation. I started to get frustrated when I felt like he refused to be clear about how a person would know they were saved. He started to get frustrated because I was so adamant that such a thing could, or should, be clear. We were talking about exactly the same thing, and totally agreed with each other. He fully believed that a person needs to have faith in Christ, but he was fully convinced that I focused so strongly on the boundary of "saved" or "not saved" that I was missing the movement toward the center. I was focused on the boundary. He was focused on the journey toward greater Christlikeness.

In contrast to the bounded set thinking that characterizes much of the church, centered set thinking may have boundaries, but is not defined by those boundaries. Bounded set thinking is all about position and definition. Centered set thinking focuses on direction and relationship. "If the objects to be organized are moving toward the center, they are considered to be in the set. ... Objects that in some sense may be considered near the center but moving away from it are seen to be outside the set. Thus, the boundary is determined by the relation of the objects to the center and not by essential characteristics of the objects themselves."[65] In the conversation with my pastor friend, it was more important that someone was moving closer to the person of Christ, than in our being able to define with certainty whether that person was "saved."

Most of that shift is quiet and subtle, like the quiet way people simply don't join a church. Some of it is neither quiet nor subtle. In many cases, bounded set thinking is being explicitly rejected by the culture around us. Mark Baker, Professor of Mission and Theology at Fresno Pacific Biblical Seminary, reflects on "...the damage done by bounded churches and the judgmental lines of division they draw," noting that "The boundary lines not only injure the excluded, but those inside as well."[66]

Much of the way the church has defined itself in the past is now seen by Baker and many others as not just outdated, but actually harmful. If you're like me, calling my way of doing church "harmful" and "wrong" raises your hackles. Church has worked just fine for hundreds of years thank you very much. And who do these people think they are to tell me that what means so much to me is judgmental and hurtful? Therein lies a huge part of the problem.

This paradigm shift from bounded to centered set thinking is creating some interesting and potentially divisive issues in the church. Most of the divisiveness has more to do with our attitudes and defensiveness than with reality. I need to stop defending myself long enough

83

to engage in real conversation with people (like my young pastor friend) who don't think like me.

One straightforward example has to do with church and denominational membership. It used to be common sense that people would become members of their churches, and churches would belong to a specific denomination. Americans in the 21st century push back against that kind of thing. "Many American believers resist being bound to any particular church or denomination based on a particular set of beliefs and rules. ... Members [used to know] what it meant to belong, and constitutions described clear processes for getting in and what would cause someone to be voted out. But those boundaries are gradually weakening."[67] Those of us who have been part of the church for many years can't imagine why they wouldn't want to join the church. They can't imagine why we'd even ask the question. The whole shift has nothing to do with core doctrine or spiritual maturity. It has everything to do with a different way of thinking.

Cultural paradigms have dramatically shifted in the 21st century and the church has to deal with that shift. Most of the power in the church lies in the hands of the older generations. It is on us to be the ones who understand the times and know what the church should do. We'll consider more of this as the book progresses, but for now I see four key things we need to do.

First, like Daniel, we need to study culture. It's not enough to watch the news and complain about the state of the nation. We need to immerse ourselves in what's going on around us. Read books, talk to people who think differently, watch news channels we don't agree with. Second, we need to remain diligent in the pursuit of our own faith. As deeply immersed as Daniel was in his efforts to understand the world around him, he never lost his focus on his own relationship with God. Third, we need to prayerfully distinguish between personal preferences and biblical principles. As one simple (but emotionally loaded) example, age-graded Sunday School classes are a personal preference for most of us; but there's nothing in the Bible about that particular approach to discipleship. Finally, we need to engage in the world around us. Our tendency is to retreat to somewhere that feels safe. We already noted that Daniel was an octogenarian when he was thrown into the lion's den. At 80 years old he was still fully engaged as a key leader at a national level.

Observe the end of that particular story as King Darius draws empire-wide attention to God because of Daniel's faith:

> Then King Darius wrote to all the nations and peoples of every language in all the earth: "May you prosper greatly! I issue a decree that in every part of my kingdom people must fear and reverence the God of Daniel. For he is the living God and he endures forever; his kingdom will not be destroyed, his dominion will never end. He rescues and he saves; he performs signs and wonders in the heavens and on the earth. He has rescued Daniel from the power of the lions." So Daniel prospered during the reign of Darius and the reign of Cyrus the Persian.[68]

Like Daniel, we find ourselves in a society that has no interest in our God. We find ourselves in a secular culture that pulls people away from God and his church. Like Daniel we need to work hard to understand that culture. Like Daniel we must never compromise our faith, but sacrifice personal preferences in favor of biblical principles. All in order that people will fear and reverence the living God.

Chapter Five

Generational Shift

Every year one of my great joys is teaching an Old Testament Survey course to a group of young men and women as part of a Discipleship School. No matter how many times I teach the course, I'm stunned every time I introduce the era of the Judges. The story leading up to that point has been pretty amazing. After their 40 year time out in the wilderness, the Hebrews are finally ready to move into the land God had promised to Abraham, Isaac and Jacob hundreds of years before.

At the end of the book of Deuteronomy Moses passes the leadership baton to Joshua. Shortly after that, in an episode filled with spiritual ritual and significance, the priests lead the people across the Jordan River. Once across, the people stop to remember what God has done to bring them to this point, and to renew their covenant with him. Then comes the first part of the conquest. In a way designed to focus attention on God, they worship him as they march around the walls of Jericho. God brings the walls down and God brings the victory. Joshua leads a brilliant military campaign, marred only by a few lapses of judgment and the occasional sin in the camp. God causes the walls to collapse at Jericho. He causes the sun to stand still in the battle against the Amorites. He causes devastating hail to fall before the enemy could regroup. Time after time God causes the Israelites to defeat fortified city states and their armies. Through it all the people know it is God doing the fighting. They build an altar out of stones from the Jordan. They build another after the victory at Ai.

Eventually we're told that "Joshua took the entire land, just as the Lord had directed Moses, and he gave it as an inheritance to Israel according to their tribal divisions. Then the land had rest from war."[69] Time passes and Joshua grows old. He calls the nation together so that he can give them his farewell address. He calls them to renew their national covenant with God and warns them against breaking that covenant. As his address comes to a close the people respond to his call:

And the people said to Joshua, "We will serve the Lord our God and obey him." On that day Joshua made a covenant for the people, and there at Shechem he reaffirmed for them decrees and laws. And Joshua recorded these things in the Book of the Law of God. Then he took a large stone and set it up there under the oak near the holy place of the Lord. "See!" he said to all the people. "this stone will be a witness against us. It has heard all the words the Lord has said to us. It will be a witness against you if you are untrue to your God."[70]

All was well while Joshua and his generation were alive. The era of the conquest gives way to the era of the Judges and things go terribly wrong:

Joshua son of Nun, the servant of the Lord, died at the age of a hundred and ten. And they buried him in the land of his inheritance, at Timnath Heres in the hill country of Ephraim, north of Mount Gaash. After that whole generation had been gathered to their ancestors, another generation grew up who knew neither the Lord nor what he had done for Israel. Then the Israelites did evil in the eyes of the Lord and served the Baals. They forsook the Lord, the God of their ancestors, who had brought them out of Egypt. They followed and worshiped various gods of the peoples around them. They aroused the Lord's anger because they forsook him and served Baal and the Ashtoreths.[71]

They "knew neither the Lord nor what he had done for Israel." No matter how many times I read that sentence I continue to be amazed. How is it possible that this generation has no idea what their parents and grandparents have experienced? How is it possible that they haven't been told what God had done? How is it possible that they haven't seen who God is through the faith of their parents? After all the altars and stones and repeated covenants so carefully orchestrated to remember, how could Joshua's generation have failed so miserably as parents?

Then I started studying 21st century cultural issues. I think now that it was likely much more complicated than poor parenting. What if Joshua's generation did tell their kids about who God was and what God had done for them? What if they faithfully lived out their faith so that their kids could see it? What if they continually marveled at the fact that God had kept his promises and blessed their nation? And what if faith and life looked so different to the next generation that their parents' stories and examples made no sense to them?

The Bible doesn't tell us exactly what happened all those millennia ago, but we're experiencing something similar in this century. This is one of those places where we need to understand the times if we're going to know what the church should do. We've already looked at the secularization of society, and at the way thinking has shifted from bounded to centered set. Now we turn our attention to what's happening as the cultural center of gravity shifts from one generation to the next.

Generations

Most of us are familiar with the concept of Baby Boomers, Busters and Millennials, but we tend to miss the implications for the church. What shaped us is not what is shaping the next generation, so it's important to have at least a basic understanding of the generational shifts going on around us. Sociologists all have their own ways of doing this, but in general there are five generations that are important for us right now. Elders were born before 1946. Their children make up the Boomer generation, born from 1946 to 1964. Boomers were followed by Generation X, also known as Busters; they were born between 1965 and 1983. Then came the Millennials, born from 1984 to 2001. This generation garnered a huge amount of attention by sociologists, historians and the business world as everyone tried to figure out what made them tick. By the time most of the church started to pay attention, we'd missed the boat and Generation Z was on the rise. Gen Z was born between 2002 and 2015.[72]

Each of these generations has its own worldview, with associated values and behaviors. If we know more about what these worldviews entail, we'll be in a better position to understand and respond in meaningful ways.

The Elder generation grew up during the Depression and World War II. They came to embrace conformity and traditional family values; and they tend to be conservative about most things in life, from finances to politics to religion. As World War II came to a close, the Elders focused on other things and set about producing and raising the Boomers, so called because of the post-war baby boom.

Boomers knew relative prosperity in the post-war era. They saw the rise and assassination of John F Kennedy and Martin Luther King. They were young people as the civil rights movement drew attention to racial inequality. They grew up watching TV, which provided a whole new window on the world. They saw the Beatles, and experienced the sex, drugs, and rock n' roll culture of the 60's. Boomers have become cynical, somewhat gloomy and distrustful of government; which is ironic since they hold the vast majority of civic and governmental leadership roles.

Gen X, or Busters, are now in their 30's and 40's. They witnessed the end of the Cold War and the destruction of the Berlin Wall. They watched MTV, experienced the early days of the internet, and celebrated the end of South African Apartheid. They display the fruit of the Boomer parenting and life style in that they experience more divorce than any other generation, expect immediate feedback, and reject rules. They are distrustful of existing institutions (including the church) and they are skeptical of their parents' values.

Generation follows generation. The Gen Xers are followed by the Millennials, now young adults. They are a racially diverse generation, 44% of this generation in America are Latino or non-white. The Millennials experienced mass shootings such as those at Columbine. They embraced the rise of social media. Their most significant experience was 9/11 and the subsequent, ongoing war on terror. They tend to expect instant gratification, be very informal, and have a short attention span. They are more culturally and racially tolerant than their parents. Unlike Boomers, they are generally optimistic about the future.

Millennials prefer a flat management and collaborative style of work, which is not how most of our churches are structured. This is particularly troubling for the next generation of pastors since both generations tend to equate church structure and theology. The older generation feels their theology is under attack, rather than their leadership style and structure. The younger generation feels that their theology is under attack because the older generation doesn't agree with their leadership style and structure. A while ago I attended a pastoral leadership seminar in California. One evening we were at an absolutely gorgeous home in the hills overlooking the city. As we had dinner out on the patio, the conversation turned to church governance and programming. It was fascinating to watch different generations of pastors trying to correct each other. It was a reminder to me that we have to work hard to understand generational differences.

Career hopping is the norm for Millennials. Staying with one job is no longer typical, with many Millennials shifting jobs and companies every three years or so. If this generation shifts jobs every three years, we should expect them to shift churches at least that frequently, if for no other reason than that they physically move to wherever their new company takes them. Think about the implications of that for a minute. Most of our churches expect people to be around for several years before they can have significant positions of leadership and responsibility within the organization. If Millennials move every three years, what happens to the development of church leaders? Once again, this is why we need to understand the culture around us. Millennials aren't going to start settling down just because we think they should. If we want them to grow into leaders who take responsibility in the church, we have to rethink the way we identify and develop leaders.

Following the Millennials, Gen Zers are starting to drive. Gen Z is growing up as the last generation in which the majority will be white, and they feel good about that. They are becoming young adults in a world of unparalleled cultural change. Gen Z has never known a time without terrorism as a central reality of life. They have never known a time where same-sex marriage was not legal, or a time when homeland security, immigration concerns, and increasing diversity were not normal. They are used to having completely individualized experiences: from personal playlists for their music, to advertising that specifically targets their interests, to customizable avatars in games. There was a time when your drink options were "regular or decaf." Last time someone counted, Starbucks offered over 87,000 different drink options. Some of us remember when we could choose from any of the three TV stations. You can now choose from thousands of movies and shows any time you want ... and that's just on Netflix.

For Gen Z, tolerance of personal differences is no longer sufficient; now one must explicitly affirm another's life and moral choices. Related to their insistence on affirmation, they reject imposed labels, particularly when it comes to sexuality: "Sexuality should be free from any and all restrictions, and people should be allowed to follow their desires, moment by moment."[73] Businesses have gone to great lengths to accommodate this generation, which is poised to account for as much as 40 percent of consumers in America. Attempting to meet the needs of Gen Z Facebook rolled out 50 gender options, including agender (someone who identifies as being without gender), cisgender (someone whose identity corresponds with their birth sex), gender fluid (someone who prefers to remain flexible with regard to their gender), and pan gender (someone who considers themselves a member of all genders). Facebook has since changed their approach, but you get the idea.

Despite how young they still are, Gen Z is having a huge impact on our culture. One Christian researcher stated it this way: "They will not simply influence American culture, as any generation would; they will constitute American culture."[74] They "...will be the most influential religious force in the West and the heart of the missional challenge facing the Christian church."[75]

At the same time, it's important to remember that "youth" isn't the point. The cultural paradigm shift is cross-generational. It is part of the fabric of our society, and not limited to a single generation or people group. It is helpful to consider generational themes, particularly those of the next generation, only insofar as younger generations seem to more obviously exhibit characteristics of the new way of thinking. And the generational shifts have some strong implications for the church.

For instance, younger adults have never known life without immediate access to the internet, but it didn't really take that long for us older adults to expect the same thing. Short attention spans, instant feedback, and constant connectivity are normative. The internet has become most peoples' primary source of knowledge. The internet is a vast collection of information that requires a person to search, sift, and synthesize material that is inconsistent and often incomplete. This contrasts sharply with traditional learning models based on a teacher (or preacher) and a textbook. When searching, sifting, and synthesizing information assumed to be inconsistent and incomplete is the primary way people learn, what happens when they go to church and we expect them to sit still for 40 minutes while a preacher tells them what to believe?

Electronics

Somewhat related to the internet discussion, a new area of study is looking at the impact of electronics on the human brain. The latest statistics show that people are now spending an average of twelve hours a day interacting with a digital device of one kind or another.[76] When I first heard that number it sounded ridiculous; probably just a number made up by some professor looking for attention. Then I considered the life of a typical high school student. The first thing they do when they wake up is reach for the phone, which is conveniently recharging on the bedside stand. They scan through their social media apps to see what their friends are doing and to make sure they didn't miss anything important while they were sleeping. While they're getting ready for school, they watch video blogs, which is where they get most of their world and consumer news, delivered by social media trendsetters (you can tell these trendsetters know what they're talking about because they have so many followers). A few minutes later they're scrolling through social media again while they wait for the school bus. On the bus they Snapchat or FaceTime or play online games with their friends. Those friends, by the way, are likely to be on the other side of the country, or in another country altogether.

Right about the time we'd expect them to put their electronics away for class, the teachers ask them to pull out their laptops. Content, textbooks, class assignments and even tests are online. During lunch they're back on social media and their online games. The cycle repeats after school: they pull out their phones and watch their favorite YouTube star while they have a snack, they binge on Netflix until they switch back to their laptops for homework. All the while they're online with friends. The day ends with more texts, tweets and snaps. In one way or another, this next generation (and many of the rest of us) are on some sort of electronic device almost all day, every day. Not surprisingly, this is having a significant impact on brain development, social interaction, and even spirituality.

As one example of the impact of electronics on brain development, consider the case of dopamine. Social media and online games are intentionally designed to require a "swipe" about every 13 seconds. Swipe to send a message, swipe to change screens, swipe to get the guys in the game, you get the idea. Every time you swipe, every time you get a text message, every time you get Facebook post, your brain releases the neurotransmitter dopamine. It's not as simple as it sounds, but dopamine is commonly thought of as the pleasure chemical. It's the same chemical associated with drug addiction. Dopamine impacts sleep, mood, attention, learning, and a whole lot of other things.

The research is still fairly new, and brain chemistry is obviously much more complex than a single example of a single neurotransmitter. We have to be careful with our conclusions. Having said that, it should come as no surprise that the early research shows that American's sharp increase in anxiety, depression, aggression and suicide is directly correlated to what science is discovering about the way our electronics impact brain chemistry. My point is not to make a value statement on digital media. As with any tool, there are pros and cons with electronics, and like it or not, smart phones, tablets and wrist devices are here to stay. My point is to draw our attention to the fact that our culture is impacted in ways most of us haven't even considered. My point is to get us thinking about the church's role in that culture. What does evangelism and discipleship look like in a digital age? We can't simply tell people to put their phones down and sit quietly while we talk. The world doesn't work that way anymore.

As the church we need to realize that this next generation does not see the world as we see it. Young people are not in some phase they're going to grow out of. I wonder if something like that happened to Joshua's generation. I wonder if those parents and grandparents never quite figured out that their kids simply didn't think, or learn, or view the world, like they did. Maybe they just kept waiting for their kids to change. I suggest we learn from them and not repeat their mistakes. And to repeat a significant point: while the issues are most striking in the younger generations, they are certainly not limited to those who are young. The vast majority of Americans are inextricably tethered to our screens. Whatever your age, every swipe of a screen produces a hit of dopamine.

Every 13 seconds for 12 hours add up to more than 3,000 dopamine hits every day. The church can't compete with that; nor should it try. But we do need to consider what that means for the way we go about engaging the people around us. Perhaps we'll need faster paced programming that accommodates shorter attention spans. We need to consider blogs and vlogs as significant ways to communicate and teach. It's tempting to try and serve as a sort of antidote to people's reliance on devices; but that misses the point. Devices are here, they're ubiquitous, and few people will be anything other than uncomfortable when those devices are being ignored. Instead, we should look for ways to capitalize on the opportunity. Using apps for content delivery could replace printed bulletins. That also saves paper in a culture where (as we'll see in the next chapter) people are deeply concerned about such things. Those same apps might be used within services and classes to provide live feedback and promote discussion. You'll likely have more ideas here than I do.

Values

As culture shifts around us, it's not surprising to discover that priorities and core values are fundamental to that shift. It's a bit more surprising to realize just how dramatically our culture's values have changed in what feels like a very short amount of time. Once again, many of us were waiting for youthful fads and idealism to give way to something more realistic and, well, more like the things Americans have valued for many, many years. Instead, philosophies or values we once held as self-evident truth, have been turned on their heads. Here are just a few that appear to be particularly significant.

Experience versus propositional truth

Arguably beginning with the modern era, logical thinking and the scientific method have played a major role in the way people think and go about life. School teachers and textbooks tell us what we should know and it's taken for granted that we should in fact know these things. It's also taken for granted that the information they provide is valid. Content is presented in the form of proposition: the teacher telling the student something that is expected to be believed because of the logic behind the statement.

The institutional church has based most of its programs around the same approach to logic and scientific method. It's with those dearly held values that we approach Sunday School classes where children (and adults) are expected to diligently learn the lesson for the day. Adult small groups often use video-driven lectures as the basis for their study. Seminarians study systematic theology and apologetics so they understand the logic and structure behind their faith. Most conspicuous is the weekly sermon, around which the weekend service invariably revolves. A typical sermon is all about propositional truth. The pastor lays out the logical case for why his or her point is to be believed. The congregation historically places the same value on propositional truth and dutifully believes what they're told.

In contrast, culture in the 21st century values experience over proposition. It's not that there's no place for logic or methodology, but particularly where personal belief is concerned, experience clearly takes precedence. People are less interested in being told what's true and more interested in experiencing truth. A recent study by the Barna Group found that "This generation wants to experience God, as well as get to know him through his Word. ... They want a Gospel that is full of power that will help them to navigate the complexities of living in this world. ... Faith for them must be dynamic, growing, moving, felt, tasted, touched, seen and heard. It must invade all of their life."[77]

Perhaps that was part of the problem with the generation after Joshua's generation had passed. Perhaps they heard their parents talk about who God is and what he's done, but they didn't have any personal experience of God.

The shift from propositional to experiential truth as a cultural value suggests that the church needs to make a similar shift. As the Barna Group survey discovered, it's not that there's no place for the Bible, but the emphasis needs to shift from pastors (and others) telling people about God to the Community of the Gospel inviting others into a life-changing experience with the living Christ.

Authenticity versus excellence

One of the most essential values in American culture today is that of authenticity. Not to be confused with integrity, which has to do with how you interact with others, authenticity has more to do with my relationship to myself. Discovering who I really am and then being true to that identity is paramount. For better or worse, that desire for authenticity explains the meteoric rise to prominence for both Colin Kaepernick and President Donald Trump. When Kaepernick knelt during the national anthem, he immediately created armies of people who were for his act as a powerful statement against systemic racism, or against it as disrespectful and unpatriotic. Both sides of that particular culture war, however, were impressed with the fact that Kaepernick was being true to himself. In other words, he was being authentic. President Trump gained prominence in part through the contrast between his style and that of his rival presidential candidates. Candidates like Mitt Romney were characterized as "stiff," while Hillary Clinton didn't "connect" with people. Trump's supporters claimed that whatever you might think about his social media comments and personal ethic, he was at least being himself. In other words, he was being authentic.

This cultural obsession with authenticity has tremendous implications for the church. First, it dictates much of what people expect from their church, whether that be ecclesia or institution. Philosopher Charles Taylor says it this way: "The religious life or practice that I become part of must not only be my choice, but it must speak to me, it must make sense in terms of my spiritual development as I understand this."[78] At one level this kind of thinking is simply a self-centered demand on others to conform to my preferences. Since authenticity is all about my true self, "The age of authenticity asserts that we should be directed by nothing outside us but only by what we find meaningful within us"[79] It only makes sense then, that my experience of church should be tailored to my own preferences and to that which I find meaningful. At the same time, this focus on self serves as a powerful reminder that how people experience church is unique to each person and does need to be personally meaningful. The onus is often on the church body to offer worship and learning experiences that afford people the opportunity to go further in their journey toward Christ. If the sermon is boring, or the setting is distracting, it may not be the individual's fault if they're not engaged.

The second implication stemming from the value of authenticity is the rejection of excellence as a church value. In previous decades, excellence was a hallmark of a good church. Worship, leadership, preaching and facility design all were done with the highest quality achievable. The thought was that Christ and his church deserved nothing less. As cultural values have shifted, excellence has become more associated with hypocrisy than with anything else. When culture holds that "It is better to be bad but authentic than to be good but phony,"[80] hypocrisy is anathema. According to a recent Barna Group study, two-thirds of Millennials "... believe American churchgoers are a lot or somewhat hypocritical (66%). To a generation that prides itself on the ability to smell a fake at 10 paces, hypocrisy is the mother of all indictments.[81] Unfortunately, Kinnamen notes, society may well be correct. "...When it came to nonreligious factors – the *substance* of people's daily choices, actions, and attitudes – there were few meaningful gaps between born-again Christians and non-born-agains."[82]

Excellence, expressed as the best we have to offer Christ, is not a bad thing. But we need to ensure that in our laudable efforts to present God our best, we are not putting a false face on the church. Excellence can never be at the expense of honesty. We cannot pretend to be something we are not. If our attitudes, actions and speech do not reflect Christ, the world has no reason to believe what they see is real. Addressing the real and perceived hypocrisy in the church, Kinnamen suggests that the church also needs to be intentionally transparent. We need to admit, and repent of, the inconsistencies in our lives and engage in dialogue that is restorative. "Instead of pretending to have all the answers, godly transparency is oriented toward helping people get their lives back in line."[83] Only then will we be able to overcome the public perception that the church is nothing more than a gathering of hypocrites.

Additional Values

Experience and authenticity are the two most fundamental values we need to understand, but there are so many more issues that are deeply important to this new culture we live in. Many of these we've touched on in other parts of this book, but so that we don't miss them, here are a few.

Diversity versus homogeneity. In an era were people are acutely aware of racial and other justice issues, anything that lacks diversity, especially racial diversity, is suspect at best. Recall too from our discussion of generational distinctives, that Gen Z is likely to be the last generation in which Anglos are in the majority; and people are more than OK with that. As one author put it: "They want more than tolerance of others; they seek an embrace of differences, valuing the beauty in difference."[84] For Christ's church to lack diversity is a powerful, negative statement to many in the 21st century.

Relational versus institutional. While not really new to the 21st century, people's emphasis on the importance of relationships, combined with their growing rejection of institutions of any kind are significant for the church. They are drawn to authentic relationships rather than an organization. A few years ago Stetzer, Stanley and Hayes published findings of a study called "Lost and Found." In the study they discovered that only one in six young people would turn to the church for spiritual help. Interestingly, in the same group, nine out of ten had a close friend who was a Christian. So as Cole asks: "why don't we switch our strategy from attractive church programming to something that empowers and releases those close Christian friends to have a real influence?"[85]

We noted already that in the 21st century people are more interested in the journey than in the destination (recall the nature of centered-set thinking). Combining that notion with the importance of relationships, we need to begin thinking of ourselves as tour guides rather than as travel agents. In the age of the internet and the immediate access it provides to people and thinking from all over the world, we increasingly think along global rather than national lines. This should impact the sensitivity with which we approach national holidays and discussion related to national politics and similar issues. Also related to the way the internet has changed the way we think, culture, particularly in younger generations, tends to think more in terms of crowd sourcing than singular authority (consider Wikipedia, which has all but replaced more traditional encyclopedias). This presents a challenge to the way traditional pastors preach and lead. Ironically, while crowd sourcing has become the new norm, the new world is also one "of 'tailored analytics' that instantly customizes [people's] online experience. This leads them to expect that everything put in front of them has been customized."[86]

In later chapters we'll visit some broad ideas regarding what the church needs to consider as we represent Christ in the 21st century, but let me make one suggestion now: it's all about relationships. The people around us are skeptical and a bit resentful. They don't see the world the way we do, and the church is perceived as irrelevant and judgmental. Most people are going to expect us to be that way: irrelevant and judgmental when it comes to spiritual things. I had a conversation not too long ago with a good pastor friend of mine. He's a godly man, wise beyond his years, and he's part of the Millennial generation. In a profoundly telling moment, he was talking about his generation when he said, "we inherited a new world and it has not been kind to us." To be honest, my first response was something like: "Buck up buttercup; the world wasn't kind to us either." I'm so glad that in my profound wisdom and deep maturity I didn't say that out loud. Rightly or wrongly, this next generation feels disrespected, they feel judged, and they feel vaguely oppressed. There's nothing in their life experience telling them how to deal with that, so telling them to "buck up" doesn't help. Add 3,000 dopamine hits every day; remember they grew up in a society that pulls them away from the things of God; know that the way they think makes traditional understandings of God and church confusing to them; and we have our work cut out for us.

So what do we do? Think "tour guide." American culture, especially but not specifically among the younger generations, values experience over proposition. That's going to involve a mindset change for many of us. The organization of the church is almost completely designed around propositional truth. We declare what truth is, support it with biblical facts, and move on. Propositional truth forms the basis for our Sunday School classes, our preaching, our missions, and for everything else. It's not that truth isn't truth any more. But it no longer works to tell people what to believe or how to behave. The people around us need to experience it for themselves. And they need to experience it in the context of authentic relationships. Rather than telling people, we need to find ways to be involved in their lives.

This gives us a great opportunity, because our new culture values relationships over institutions. They're not going to come find us in church. At best they're not interested. We need to go to where they are in order to begin those authentic relationships. Think back to our discussion of centered sets. In centered set thinking the journey is more important than the destination. Rather than acting as travel agents who tell people where to go and how to get there, we need to act as tour guides, walking alongside them, sharing our experience, and allowing them to experience the journey toward Christ for themselves.

We need to go into those relationships with more questions than answers. We need to listen more than we talk. We need to love more than defend. We need to experience the journey with them more than we need to drag them along a path. Sounds like what Jesus did with his own disciples doesn't it?

Chapter Six

Priority Shift

I mentioned earlier that a couple of years ago I had the opportunity to travel to South Africa and Uganda looking for some new ministry opportunities with my church. I love that kind of thing, especially when I can see positive results from the travel, exploration and new relationships. We covered a lot of ground on this particular trip. One day I was in a nice car racing down the road in an upscale Johannesburg neighborhood, chatting with the dean of a seminary. Not that long before I had been sitting on a rickety chair in a leaky shack in the slums of Cape Town, joining a neighborhood Bible study. A couple of days later I was having a great meal and some deep conversation with a Catholic priest outside Kampala.

South Africa and Uganda are both nations that have gone through horrendous levels of oppression and injustice in our own generation. Most of us are familiar with South Africa's apartheid and its segregation and oppression and violence. We know about Nelson Mandela, the champion of equality and justice there. We're probably less familiar with the brutality that took place in Uganda under Idi Amin. That was back in the '70's. Right about the time folks in America were listening to the Bee Gee's, Idi Amin was killing as many as 500,000 of his own people. That Catholic priest I met in Uganda took us to visit some of his congregation as part of our exploration. After that great meal at his home, I spent some time in a tiny little mud home and listened as an amazing older lady told stories about how her own children had been killed in the fields just beyond her house. Having that wonderful woman hold my hands while she told me her personal story of the war and brutality she lived through gave me a whole new perspective on that part of history. Uganda, like most nations, has a long way to go, but it is healing and growing and moving forward as a nation.

In our generation America hasn't suffered under quite the same kind of oppressive political regimes as have South Africa and Uganda. But pay attention to history and to the news and you quickly realize that we have plenty of our own problems with justice. Both church and non-church leaders are drawing attention to things like racism, social inequity, gender bias, and a long list of other injustices that are part of our own culture. In part I think this is a healthy, growing awareness of the need for justice. In part, it reflects a shift in our culture's priorities. One of the things I love about the Bible is that it talks about real life and real issues. As you can imagine, justice is one of those issues. The Bible talks about justice a lot actually, and it tells us two things. First, it tells us what we already know: injustice is an evil part of the world. No surprise there. But the Bible also tells us that while injustice is part of the fallen world around us, as followers of Christ, we are not to put up with it. We are to be people of justice.

The prophet Hosea says this: "But you must return to your God; maintain love and justice, and wait for your God always."[87] Another prophet, Zechariah, says much the same thing: "This is what the LORD Almighty said:

'Administer true justice; show mercy and compassion to one another. Do not oppress the widow or the fatherless, the foreigner or the poor. Do not plot evil against each other.'"[88]

There are dozens of passages like that. Time after time, God reminds his people that he is a God of justice and we need to be people of justice. We're obviously not going to try to look at all those passages here. I want to focus on one of them; the words of a man named Micah.

Micah was a prophet who lived around 700 BC. He was just a country boy from a little town called Moresheth not too far from what we now know as the Gaza strip in Israel. Academics like to say that Micah was "born of obscure parentage," which is a fancy way of saying that we don't know who his parents were, or what his background was.

Whatever his background, as Micah writes, he's furious about the oppression and injustice he sees in his nation. He's especially angry at the leaders. He refers to them as people who made straight paths crooked. He talks about judges that can be bribed, pastors who can be bought, and rulers who lay awake at night planning how they can get rich through fraud and theft:

> Woe to those who plan iniquity,
> to those who plot evil on their beds!
> At morning's light they carry it out
> because it is in their power to do it.
> They covet fields and seize them,
> and houses, and take them.

They defraud people of their homes,
they rob them of their inheritance.[89]

To make things worse, these same judges and pastors and leaders put on a very righteous front. They're apparently under the impression that they can do whatever they want as long as they also act religious. They go to church, more precisely the Temple, to make their sacrifices and look all spiritual, then they go back out and defraud someone of their life savings.

Towards the end of the book Micah asks a rhetorical question. Keep in mind that in the Old Testament worship included the sacrifice of animals to symbolically pay the penalty for sin. Olive oil was given to the Temple as part of people's offering.
With what shall I come before the LORD
and bow down before the exalted God?
Shall I come before him with burnt offerings,
with calves a year old?
Will the LORD be pleased with thousands of rams,
with ten thousand rivers of olive oil?
Shall I offer my firstborn for my transgression,
the fruit of my body for the sin of my soul?[90]

In other words, Micah says: "you think God is happy when you act all religious on Sunday?" And he builds from normal to totally ridiculous. "You think God is happy because you come to church and bow? Or you bring the perfect, year-old calf as a sacrifice? Or wait, let's up that: you bring thousands of rams! Or better yet: ten thousand rivers of oil! Or the ultimate: you sacrifice your own child to pay for your sins! Then God will be happy?"

The answer that would have been obvious to the people in Micah's time was "Of course not." Worshipping is right and good. Giving generously to God is right and good. But at the end of the day God isn't really focusing on how much money we give, or how righteous we look. God is interested in our hearts and in the action that stems from our hearts. After Micah reaches the end of that hysterical rant "let's offer ten thousand rivers worth of oil to show how generous we are!" you can feel his tone soften. "Come on people, you already know what God wants."

> He has shown you, O mortal, what is good.
> And what does the LORD require of you?
> To act justly and to love mercy
> and to walk humbly with your God.[91]

God is not impressed when I put a huge check in the offering plate if my heart isn't right. I can come to church and put on my reverent face, and say all the right things, and open my Bible every Sunday and still be missing the point. What God really wants is that we act justly, and love mercy, and walk humbly with him. As a quick aside, notice that God expects all three of those things from us: justice, mercy, and humility. I know of some people who only like the humble part. "I'm just a humble guy, walking with God. Not much I can do about all the sin in the world." There are also a few activists out there who are all over the justice part, but don't have much in the way of mercy or humility. As we focus right now on the issue of justice, keep in mind that justice, mercy, and humility go hand in hand.

For a variety of reasons, cultural priorities have shifted toward issues of justice. There are three strands of this at play as we look at society: social justice, individual justice and environmental justice.

Social Justice

In American right now people rightly want justice on a wide array of issues. Poverty alleviation, access to adequate health care, immigration concerns, the plight of refugees and the list goes on. In high school my kids were taught about faithism, ageism, homophobia (now called heterosexism) and other social ills. Racism, sexism and financial inequity are generally at the top of that long list. People keenly feel the injustice that's part of our society, and they passionately want to correct that wrong. But no one seems to know how to go about fixing things. So we miss true justice and end up with victimization, narcissism, and retribution.

Here are a couple of quick examples so we have a sense of the enormity of the concern.

The role of women in the world around us has changed dramatically in the past several years. Women now make up 57 per cent of the work force.[92] At the same time, people are still concerned about fair pay and equal opportunities for promotion, so there's an intentional effort to shatter what used to be known as "the glass ceiling." That effort includes the push to have more women CEO's in business and in key positions of political power. There's an overt demand for more strong female lead characters on TV and in action movies. I could go on.

While there has been that dramatic change in the way American values and promotes women, there has not been a similar change in the church's approach towards women. And people are paying attention. Some scholars suggest that one reason over 40 per cent of American women do not attend church is because of that disparity. Christine Caine is a Christian author who says this: "Women often feel more esteemed, valued, celebrated, and included outside of the church than within the church."[93] It seems to me that whatever the Bible teaches about women in church leadership, the church should be a place that sets the bar for valuing and celebrating women.

On the issue of racism: a recent study by the Barna Group found that 84 per cent of Americans believe that there is a lot of anger and hostility between different racial groups.[94] The only real surprise there is that 16 per cent of Americans apparently aren't aware of the tension. Given my growing concern over the chasm between church and culture, I was, though, surprised to learn that more than half of people who do not attend church think the church has a positive role to play in racial reconciliation. Disturbingly, at the same time, over 60 per cent of the population believes that the Christian church is part of the problem.[95] Unfortunately, a large number of Evangelicals believe that racism is a thing of the past. What that means is that the church, the people who should be best equipped for something like racial reconciliation and justice, doesn't think there's a problem. The Barna Group study comments: "This is a dangerous reality for the modern church. Jesus and his disciples actively sought to affirm and restore the marginalized and obliterate divisions between groups of people. Yet, our churches and ministries are still some of the most ethnically segregated institutions in the country."[96] Whatever we believe about racism, the world around us sees us as a key part of the problem when we should be part of the solution.

One more example: two-thirds of Americans believe the church should play a major role in alleviating poverty. Young people are even more adamant: almost 90 per cent of Millennial Christians believe the church should play that role.[97] In fact, with pretty much every social justice issue on the table, including poverty, young Christians want the church to lead. They want us to address racism and sexism, they want us to funnel resources outward rather than inward; they want us to talk about things like gender and identity. They desperately want us to deal with the issues that our culture is dealing with. They deeply believe we should do all those things, but they don't think we will.

It's a sad thing to be confronted with the reality that people in our culture look at the church as part of the problem of social injustice. It's even more sad to realize that our own church-going young people agree. There's no good excuse for that. Where we're not bringing the Bible to bear on culture we need to make that happen. We also need to make sure people know where we are making a difference. In days gone by, we placed a high value on anonymity and not letting "the left hand know what the right hand is doing."[98] So many of church ministries that address issues like poverty are done with little fanfare. But in an age of social media and crowd sourcing, people have a different expectation and need to know. In my own church we have a really strong benevolence ministry. Every year we give thousands of dollars to help people pay bills, buy groceries, and take care of their families. But we do it very quietly and very few in our church or community have any idea how much we help. I think we need to find some ways to tell stories of life change and church involvement. Not for bragging rights, but so that the people who make up our local body will know they're part of a church that really does address the issues they're concerned about. It's a tough balance, but perhaps we've become so concerned about humility that we're missing opportunities to draw positive attention to Christ.

Individual Justice

The second of three major strands of justice concern in our culture is that of individual justice. Most of us are familiar with the notion of individualism. Rightly or wrongly, we've grown up with the belief that we are each unique, that we should be free to make our own decisions, and that we should be independent, self-reliant. Individuals should be free to pursue their dreams and personal advancement; being equally free to enjoy the fruit of success or the responsibility of failure. Individualism as we've understood it is quietly giving way to a new philosophy. I'm not sure it has a real, culturally agreed upon name, so let's call it neo-individualism.

Neo-individualism takes all the uniqueness and freedoms demanded by individualism and builds on them. Neo-individualism believes that humans have the right to make their own, individual decisions about what it means not just to pursue their own dreams, but what it means to be human. White asserts that "Ours is the generation that will be forced to examine and elucidate the doctrine of humanity in ways that confront both changing morals and new technological frontiers."[99] Both personal identity and meaning are to be found within. One best-selling author notes that "...if I really pay attention and strive to get in touch with myself, I am bound to discover deep inside a single, clear and authentic voice, which is my true self, and which is the source of all meaning and authority in the universe."[100]

What makes this a cultural thing (rather than just a few philosophic rebels) is the related belief that our individual decisions about human expression can only be truly realized when others affirm our choices. We are at the point in society where not only am I free to define myself any way I want, you are obligated to agree with, and even celebrate, my definition. Along those lines Mark Yarhouse, a leading Christian scholar on gender dysphoria, comments that society is rapidly moving to a position which "sees the reality of transgender persons as something to be celebrated, honored, or revered. ... some wish to recast sex as just as socially constructed as gender."[101] Certainly not limited to sexual identity, the expectation that others will celebrate my personal life definitions is readily apparent in social media, where much of the dialogue has to do with giving and receiving affirmation of our life choices.

We noted in a previous chapter that authenticity is a strong value in our culture. As authenticity encounters neo-individualism, if I'm going to be truly authentic, I need to get rid of anything that might be hindering my journey toward my authentic self. Thus absolutes of gender, moral codes, institutional loyalty, even God, should be disregarded. Perhaps better said: any of those things should be considered fluid; they should be able to change and flow whenever it's most convenient. And of course, you are still obligated to affirm me and my decisions as I journey toward my authentic self.

I might choose to believe in God, not because the person of God is an objective reality that demands a response, but because the concept of God is satisfying or rewarding or useful to me. Since I don't believe in God as an objective reality, it doesn't matter if I change my mind later. The same thing is true of church. I might choose to attend church with no sense that there's a moral or spiritual reality behind it. My choice to attend is based on my perception of value: I attend because I get something in return. If I find no value in attending, that's fine too. Believing in God, or not believing in God, are equally valid, personal choices, and society is required to affirm either choice as long as that choice is an authentic expression of my individual self. Of course, the cultural bell-curve of secularization pushes against church attendance. Culture says that I should not attend church, and if I do, you should not affirm that particular choice. Such is America in the 21st century.

Environmental Justice

Americans are deeply concerned about both social and individual justice. They are equally concerned about environmental justice, that is, the way we care for our planet. Many consider deforestation, animal species on the brink of extinction, reliance on non-renewable energy, and similar things to be issues of justice. Climate change is the current hot button, raising angst on both sides of the discussion. Most Americans firmly believe that climate change is very real and that humanity is responsible for it. As we saw with issues of race, the general population of the United States has significant differences of opinion with those of the evangelical church. Only 21 per cent of Americans believe that climate change is "probably" or "definitely" not the fault of us humans. 42 per cent of evangelicals believe that humans have "definitely not" caused climate change.[102]

Norman Wirzba, professor of theology and ecology at Duke University, is one of the most prominent Christian writers on the topic of environmental justice. His arguments exemplify the shift in thinking among Christian leaders and theologians:

Put practically, Jesus shows us that the primary task of discipleship is for people to be a healing, nurturing, and reconciling presence in the world. When creatures are degraded, as they clearly are when animal livestock are kept in close stifling confinement (all so that we can have cheap meat), or when mountains are blown to hell (all so that coal and electricity can be provided more cheaply), Christians are called to protest and protect the sanctity of life that is there under attack. They are called to implement and model ways of producing food and packaging energy that honor the goodness and beauty of creatures. When this happens, Christians will in fact be 'good news' to other creatures because they will be in the world in ways that are sympathetic and harmonious. They will be ministers of a gospel that has been 'proclaimed to every creature under heaven' (Col. 1:23).[103]

Ranging from the cellular to the atmospheric levels, there is no place or process on Earth that does not reflect humanity's technological prowess and its economic reach. ... then it is of the utmost importance that we submit this power to rigorous examination. So much – perhaps everything – is at stake."[104]

With new theological approaches and new cultural priorities staring us in the face, it's wise to revisit the biblical basis for our response. Adam and Eve were placed in the Garden and given the instruction to "subdue" the earth, to eat the plants and to rule over the animals.[105] In the modern era we routinely focused on our own understanding of terms like "subdue" and "rule" without paying much attention to the real meaning of those words. As the Bible continues, it restates the point: "The Lord God took the man and put him in the Garden of Eden to work it and take care of it."[106] Humans have been given the ability to enjoy the beauty and goodness of God's creation. We have also been given the responsibility to "work it and take care of it." In 21st century parlance we'd likely say that humanity has been given the responsibility to steward creation. As history progressed, sin entered creation, making that stewardship a burden as well as a joy. But the mandate to steward God's creation has never been revoked.

Cory Maxwell-Coghlan, senior writer at the Barna Group concludes:

> Faith leaders especially must be wary of hammering the stake deeper into the chasm separating those on either side of the issue. They must be willing to occupy that 'messy middle,' urging their divided congregations to look beyond their seemingly irreconcilable differences to seek common ground over a shared concern for God's creation. Whether human-caused or not, seeking energy independence, preserving rainforests, creating more livable cities, and fighting for clean water and air are all good reasons to build coalitions across political and religious divides.[107]

As we seek to be people who champion justice in the 21st century, we need to enliven our own sense of responsibility with regard to God's charge for us to steward his creation. We need to find ways to make that part of the way we "do" church as both community and organization. In this digital age for example, we can reduce our reliance on print media. With the proliferation of affordable apps, do we really need to hand out paper bulletins? It should not be that difficult to create composting and recycling opportunities, and to use eco-friendly cleaning products. Community gardens on our properties and energy efficient lighting in our buildings are also possibilities. Simple efforts like these should be part of our own sense of responsibility, but they also speak volumes to the world around us.

Think back to the prophet Micah's instruction. Notice that it's not about the absence of oppression; a righteous life embodies and encourages justice. Act justly, love mercy, walk humbly. These are not passive words. He doesn't say "avoid oppression; try really hard not to oppress anyone." He says "act justly." God wants me to be a person who acts justly. It's not enough for me to be content that I don't oppress anyone. It's not enough for me to watch the news and lament the awful things that are done in the world. I need to be a champion for justice.

I write something like that and then spend some time watching the news. It's easy to get totally overwhelmed. Racism, sexism, a refugee crisis of staggering proportions, immigration, gender choices, poverty, bigotry, abuse ... Once you start paying attention it gets really big, really fast doesn't it? How do we wrap our hearts and our minds around the immense injustice that's part of our world? How can the body of Christ even begin to right the wrongs? And how do we deal with this all in a way that makes sense to a world that thinks we should be leading the charge but doesn't believe we will?

The priorities of the world around us have shifted toward issues of justice. Not surprisingly in a fallen world justice has been confused with victimization, retribution, and covered over with a healthy dose of narcissism. At the same time, this new set of priorities gives the church an incredible opportunity for meaningful conversations and activities that can draw positive attention to Christ.

Given the immensity of the issue, let me make a couple of comments as we draw this chapter to a close. First, regardless of what the world around is interested in, God's people are called to be just. We need to take up that challenge, not because the world is interested, but because we're called to do so. We need to get out there and we need to start addressing the injustice around us. That doesn't mean we need to be angry activists (on the contrary, Micah calls us to show justice with mercy, in humility). It does mean we need to do something. As individuals and as the church, sitting on the sidelines is not an option.

Second, God does not expect me (or you) to solve all the world's problems. Nor does God expect my local church body to lead the charge on every issue that gets raised. God does expect us to do our respective parts.

This Psalmist says this:

> Take delight in the LORD,
> and he will give you the desires of your heart.[108]

This verse is often misunderstood. It does not mean that God is going to give me whatever I desire. This verse is talking about the fact that God has put inside of each of us some areas that we're passionate about. Some things that we're deeply concerned about. When we're following him, those things that we really want down deep in our souls, those are desires he's put there and wants us to act on. Knowing that, the question becomes: what area of injustice just pokes at me? What's the thing that makes me want to just get off the couch and do something about? That's probably the thing God wants me to actually do something about. And it's going to be different for each of us.

I have a friend in California who produces movies. A few years ago Jim got really fired up about the evil of sex trafficking. He travelled, he researched, he networked, and he ended up producing a movie called "Trade of Innocents." He didn't try to deal with refugees, or terrorism, or poverty, or racism. The desire God put on his heart had to do with stopping sex trafficking. So he acted. And by acting he not only helped deal with that particular injustice, he also made me that much more aware of the issue and that much more open to acting justly myself.

I have another friend who has a deep, passionate concern about the refugee crisis. Greg's not trying to fix sex trafficking, or terrorism, or malaria, although he cares about those things. The desire God put on his heart has to do with the refugee crisis. So he acted. He traveled; he researched; he networked. And as a result, not only has he helped that particular situation, he's also championed the cause of justice in a way that makes others more inclined to get involved; more inclined to act justly.

My daughter is part of a church in Phoenix that is aggressively involved in addressing the needs of inner city children around them. I know of another church that throws a huge amount of energy into adopting orphans. My own church is involved in promoting asset based community development: helping people learn to use their own resources, solve their own problems, and improve the physical, emotional, spiritual and social health of entire communities.

None of these people are trying to do it all, they just stopped long enough to figure out what God is asking them to do. Then they set about doing it.

I'm not likely to produce a multi-million-dollar movie anytime soon. Nor am I likely to take on the world's refugee crisis. But the desire God's put on my heart is to help the church be all it can possibly be to represent God's love and wholeness and reconciliation in a world that's pretty much a disaster. It's why I'm an Executive Pastor. It's why I speak and consult.

Some of us can make huge, visible contributions. Some of us are going to make contributions that most people will never know about. All of us are called to act justly. When we do that, two things are going to happen: We're going to be the kind of people and church God is calling us to be, and the world is going to take note.

Section Three

Power shifts, generational shifts, technological shifts, value shifts, paradigm shifts ... we often content ourselves with diagnosing the problem, or perhaps with just railing against the things we don't like. All the while we fight to return to the good old days when everything was done the way everything was supposed to be done. Ed Stetzer astutely noted: "The world is filled with people who will stand on the sidelines and point out the problems."[109] As we recall from the men of Issachar though, we need to both understand the times and know what to do. Thus far we've considered what Scripture says about the foundation of the church. We've looked at some of the key trends in culture. We now turn our attention to some fundamental shifts the church needs to make as we seek to be the Community of the Gospel we're called to be.

Most of us assume that the church needs to rethink its methodology so we, as the church, are better prepared to engage a lost and hurting next generation. Unfortunately, that assumption misses the mark on at least two counts. First, the conversation is not ultimately about a new generation, although that's certainly a part of the discussion. The conversation we must have is about the church of Jesus Christ and how we can best live out our responsibility in a new cultural paradigm; a paradigm that crosses generational lines. Second, it's reasonable to realize that it will take some new tools to engage meaningfully with a new culture. But it's not first the tools we need to rethink. Rather, we need to first rethink the nature and culture of the church and the world in which we find ourselves. Only then should we consider methodology.

In chapter seven we look at the earliest expression of the church. In Acts chapter 2 Luke gives us a description of that early church that's as challenging as it is brief. The description is 2,000 years old, but if we don't get this part right, everything else we do is just going to be band-aids covering a much deeper problem. In chapter eight we move on to look at some of the ways we can equip people to be live and proclaim the Gospel in the 21st century. If we're going to be the Community of the Gospel Peter talked about, if we're going to proclaim and live that Gospel as we're called to do, we're going to need to be intentional about engaging the society we live in. We conclude in chapter nine as we consider what that might look like.

Chapter Seven

Embracing our Responsibility

The answer to the immense new, and not-so-new, challenges we face in the 21st century is not more church programming; or more pastors and missionaries; or even more money. There are, however, a number of things we, the church, must do. I say that with some hesitation because we (at least I) tend to focus on the "doing" of church. It's not about "doing." While there are lots of things to do, our first responsibility is to "be" the church. We've so busy "doing" church that we've forgotten to "be" the church. We saw earlier how Peter describes ecclesia as the Community of the Gospel, a people centered on the Person of Christ. If we are to embrace our responsibility to be the church Peter described, we must relearn what it means to live as that Community of the Gospel. We must relearn what it means to proclaim that Gospel. We must relearn what it means to live that Gospel in ways the world can recognize. One of the clearest descriptions of what that looks like comes from the book of Acts.

It's Pentecost, one of the most significant celebrations on the Jewish calendar. Shortly before his ascension, Jesus had told his followers to wait. He had promised something new, something profound. He had promised that the Holy Spirit will come to them as the helper, the counselor, the one who will empower them to live as his followers, the one who will enable them to live as the

Community of the Gospel. And they waited for what must have seemed like forever. I imagine it was a mix of fear and optimism: what if they'd misunderstood? What if there was no "helper?" What if they hadn't misunderstood? Then what? Finally, as promised, the Holy Spirit comes with power. These amazed followers of Jesus leave the room they've been in and start sharing the good news of Jesus.

Jerusalem is packed to overflowing with Jews and converts to Judaism from all over the Roman empire: from India to Ethiopia, from Arabia to Spain, and from all points in between. All are there to celebrate Passover. When Jesus' followers begin to talk people quickly realize they are all hearing this astounding message in their own heart languages. We're told that they are "amazed and perplexed because "we hear them declaring the wonders of God in our own tongues!"[110] Peter moves to the front of the group and preaches a profound sermon, pointing to the person of Jesus: "Therefore let all Israel be assured of this: God has made this Jesus, whom you crucified, both Lord and Messiah."[111] As the message sinks in, 3,000 people determine to follow Christ. Then we read that this new ecclesia, this new Community of the Gospel

> ... devoted themselves to the apostles' teaching and to fellowship, to the breaking of bread and to prayer. Everyone was filled with awe at the many wonders and signs performed by the apostles. All the believers were together and had everything in common. They sold property and possessions to give to anyone who had need. Every day they continued to meet together

in the temple courts. They broke bread in their homes and ate together with glad and sincere hearts, praising God and enjoying the favor of all the people. And the Lord added to their number daily those who were being saved.[112]

In that very first sentence there are five different Greek words that describe what the people are doing. The rest of the passage is a bit like color commentary – it adds detail and shows what happens when the first five things are in place.

We're told that the people "devoted themselves to the apostles' teaching." Before we get to the word translated "teaching," we need to notice that "they devoted themselves." This little phrase sets the tone for everything that follows. The Greek word is "proskarterountes," from a root word meaning constant, enduring, persistent. The way the term is used here draws attention to the constant effort the people put toward these things. They aren't just devoted to the teaching part. They're devoted to the apostles' teaching, to fellowship, to the breaking of bread, and to prayer. We're separated by two-thousand years, but that separation in time does not change the nature of ecclesia. We are the same Community of the Gospel, the same people centered on Jesus. This first expression of ecclesia shows us what it looks like to embrace our responsibility as Christ's ecclesia. It starts with proskarterountes: a preoccupation with becoming more and more of the church Christ intends. It's a preoccupation that persists in moving closer to Jesus as the center of his church.

They've devoted themselves to four things. First, to the apostles' teaching. The Greek word here is "didache." We tend to read this sentence as if it were written in the 21st century, with all the trappings of a stereo-typical 21st century institution. We picture an adult Bible class where people are diligently taking notes as an apostle explains what the Bible means. But didache can mean both the teaching itself and the content that's being taught. The two meanings are not mutually exclusive. Putting the definition of the words together with the setting and context of the passage, what this really means is that both the teaching and the content are in view for that early church. These early Christians are not only committed to learning what the apostles had to say, they were equally committed to living it out.

One of Jesus' last commands to his disciples was that they should teach people "to obey everything I have commanded you."[113] The command isn't merely to "teach them everything," but to teach them to "obey" everything. That seems to be exactly what's happening here. It's not about content acquisition: seeing how much we can learn. The whole point of learning is so that our lives can reflect what we've learned. That takes devotion, persistence, intense effort. As this brand new Community of the Gospel, this ecclesia, gets its start the awestruck new believers are living the Gospel (remember anastrophen from chapter two).

They are committed to learning and living what the apostles' taught, and next we're told they are committed to fellowship. This isn't your basic average pot luck in a big room at "church." This is a more about doing life together. The term is "koinonia," and it has to do with having something in common. In the first century Luke's readers would likely have associated the word with "communion [fellowship] with a god."[114] Theologian James Boice explains that "...Christian fellowship means 'common participation in God'." He goes on to say: "So because they were in Jesus Christ and in God the Father, they quite naturally participated in a common life and shared everything with one another."[115] In other words, because of their common bond in Christ, they are doing life together. Not just a mid-week supper at church together; life together. A little later in the passage Luke tells us that they met together every day in the Temple courts and ate together in their homes.

Times change, culture shifts, but people are people wherever and whenever they are from. I imagine that as the excitement of the first couple of weeks starts to wear off, it gets more difficult to meet together every day. It probably feels more burdensome to have people over to dinner day after day. Doing life together isn't easy. It requires persistent effort in both the first century and the 21st century. But it's an essential part of embracing our responsibility.

Luke moves on to tell us that they are devoted to the "breaking of bread" and to "prayer." It's possible to combine these two ideas and view them as an expression of fellowship. Since their life together is precisely because of their shared relationship with Jesus communion and prayer would naturally flow from that commonality. Scholars differ on this one, but it seems most likely that Luke is keeping the ideas separate to draw attention to their significance.

"The breaking of bread" is expressed by the phrase "te klasei tou artou." We know from what follows in this passage that the believers share meals together, and in the context of life together centered on Christ, their meals include celebration of Communion. This particular phrase places the emphasis on the Communion. "Obviously, there is more than merely having one's meals with one another. This eating together was an aspect of their common loyalty to Jesus Christ."[116] Once again we need to look past our own culture to see what Luke is telling us. We eat together with friends occasionally. They do it routinely. We celebrate Communion in formal church settings once a month (some of us more often, some less). They celebrate Communion as part of their regular meals. This doesn't necessarily mean that those of us in the 21st century are required to eat in each others' homes every night, or that we must have a formal expression of Communion every time we have dinner. The implication is that sharing meals as a routine part of ecclesia should become the norm rather than the exception. Because we share a common bond in Christ, those meals (and everything else we do together) take on a significant spiritual meaning. We should take advantage of those times together to explicitly focus on our common bond in Christ.

In addition to shared meals centered on the bond they have in Christ, Luke tells us that the church in the first century is devoted to prayer. The Greek here is "tais proseuchais," which is perhaps best translated by "the prayers." Primarily made up of Jews and Jewish converts at this point in history, and *"The prayers* which the disciples shared in were probably not limited to the prayers of the Christian community only, but likely included as well the Jewish prayer at their stated hours."[117] To have prayer noted as one of the four key elements of the early church is a helpful, if challenging, reminder to those of us in the 21st century. As we strive to embrace our responsibility as the church, it's important that we incorporate all four of these elements in our own lives and worship.

Luke summarizes the early church in that single sentence: "they devoted themselves to the apostles' teaching and to fellowship, to the breaking of bread and to prayer." He continues by mentioning some of the specific attitudes and activities that grow out of those four elements. These attitudes and activities are inextricably woven together into a tapestry picturing Jesus as the Jewish Messiah, the one in whom we can place our faith. Tightly bound to the Jewish religion, it was still a new way of being. The few short sentences Luke offers provide a huge amount of insight and fodder for discussion. Four things stand out as being particularly helpful.

First, believers in this first expression of church have a clear sense of expectancy most Christians in 21st century America do not share. Luke tells us that "everyone was filled with awe." Whether "wonders and signs" are specific miracles we should expect in our own time is hotly debated. Fortunately for us, that's not the key piece for us to worry about here anyway. The important part for us is to note that the first church is filled with awe. As the passage continues it become apparent, although not explicit, that everyone fully expects God to do amazing things. In part, that expectation seems to spur on what comes next: God is and will continue doing great things, so it only makes sense that life will be different. Imagine the anticipation that comes every time they meet in the Temple courts. What's God going to do today? Who's going to join us this day? In the 21st century we need to regain that sense of awe. Recall that one of the primary values of this new culture is that of experience. People are more interested in experiencing the transforming power of the Gospel than they are in hearing about it. We need to live in anticipation of what God is going to do today. We need to be excited about who God is going to bring into the church as he draws them to himself.

Second, Luke describes a profound commonality among the church. Notice his emphasis on togetherness: "They were together," "Every day they continued to meet together," "They broke bread in their homes and ate together." Some of this would have come from the unusual circumstances they found themselves in. Remember that many of these new believers had made the pilgrimage to Jerusalem to celebrate Passover. And then they stayed. For many then, this isn't their home. They don't yet have jobs or homes of their own. There are no such things as welfare, or unemployment benefits, or government housing. So they stayed with other believers, greatly increasing their time together as well as deepening their bond in Christ. Many, perhaps most, of them are from Jerusalem. With that great sense of anticipation, they willingly shared their homes, their food, and other resources. As things got tight, they sold what they had in order to provide for each other. And through it all they had "glad and sincere hearts." That sense of commonality and the generosity it generates is not something that the church in America does well. Perhaps stemming from the individualism that's been part of American values, we don't often give up our own resources for someone else. We assume the government, or the institutional church, or just someone else, will take responsibility. In the first century church, at least those believers who were from Jerusalem still had their own lives to attend to, complete with jobs, families and friends. And yet they made time on a daily basis to be involved in each other's lives. Authenticity is a keenly felt value in the 21st century. And it is a necessary component of the profound community Luke describes in the first century church: they were devoted to the fellowship. As we persist in our efforts to live life together, that kind of generosity will begin to flow more easily.

Luke also describes worship as a vital component of that early church. They meet at the temple every day. It's hard to imagine going to church every day, even for a little while. Yet that's exactly what they're doing. In addition to everything else they have going on in their daily lives, they make time to meet together in the temple. Presumably this included the prayers they were devoted to. It would also have been a good place for people to gather to hear from the apostles. Worship also has an informal component as they eat together in homes. Given their glad and sincere hearts, it's not hard to imagine them finishing a great meal; the meal logically (for them) ends with a time of Communion around the dinner table, and then someone starts to sing even as they sit there. Two-thousand years later most of us struggle just to get to a Bible study group every couple of weeks. While we're there we don't generally stay for more than an hour or two, certainly not enough time for a good dinner followed by Communion; to say nothing of persistent prayer. That's one of the things we need to figure out if we're going to embrace our responsibility to be the church. We noted earlier that 21st century culture values relationship over institution. We need to find ways to do life together, with an explicit component of worshipping together as a routine part of that shared life.

Finally, after pointing out the sense of expectation that is part of their life together and which includes both formal and informal worship, Luke lets us know what was happening outside the church. As these amazing, devoted, Jewish followers of Jesus do life together, centering that togetherness on the person of Christ, others notice. At least initially people are impressed. Luke says they enjoyed "the favor of all the people." Apparently the glad and sincere hearts, the generosity and the togetherness all commanded a kind of respect. Based on the broader narrative of Acts the church is also not hesitant to verbally proclaim the Gospel. Just a few pages further in Luke's writing he mentions that even as persecution begins to rear its ugly head "they spoke the word of God boldly."[118] And as others see the Gospel lived out, as they hear the Gospel proclaimed and as they witness what the Community of the Gospel really looks like, they get it. Luke concludes this section of his work by exclaiming: "And the Lord added to their number daily those where being saved."

Despite the fact, or more likely because of the fact, that the early church enjoys so much public favor, it doesn't take long for religious leaders and others to become jealous, which sparks first an attempt to shut them up, and then a full-fledged persecution. Even once it starts to get rough, Luke makes sure we know that

All the believers were one in heart and mind. No one claimed that any of their possessions was their own, but they shared everything they had. With great power the apostles continued to testify to the resurrection of the Lord Jesus. And God's grace was so powerfully at work in them all that there were no needy persons among them. For from time to time those who owned land or houses sold them, brought the money from the sales and put it at the apostles' feet, and it was distributed to anyone who had need.[119]

Embracing our responsibility as the church in the 21st century begins when we follow the example of that early church. Luke doesn't tell us how they organized their teaching (that didn't likely evolve until later), or who took care of the kids (the littlest were likely running around the house playing while the others joined the group), or who was in charge of the benevolence program (that also comes later). Luke simply makes sure we know the basics. Our biggest challenge may be looking past the programs and processes we've created so that we can see those basics.

Not too long ago I found myself sitting in a state conference on substance abuse and mental health. It isn't a Christian conference by any stretch of the imagination, but participants and presenters alike were passionately seeking ways to help people find wholeness and health. The speaker of the hour is talking about the need for relationships in order for us to be resilient people in a time of change and stress.[120] His presentation has nothing to do with church, but his well-researched and articulate presentation leads him to the conclusion that resilience is only the second most powerful thing. The first, he goes on, is unconditional love. He attributes the idea to the Beatle's classic "All You Need is Love." Wrong attribution; right idea. As he continues, he convinces his audience that "someone needs you and you need them." The more of those relationships we have the more resilience we have.

Unintentionally, the speaker is arguing part of Luke's point and perhaps pulling the curtain back a bit on the first century church. We're not, he says, designed to be Lone Rangers. We're designed for community. Luke reminds us that the church is designed to be that community. A community centered on the person of Christ, the epitome of unconditional love. If we function as God intended his ecclesia to function, as the Community of the Gospel, we'll be doing everything this speaker could only theorize about in his quest to help people be healthy and whole.

In the 21st century we need to devote ourselves, to persist, to endure in the pursuit of those same things they devoted themselves to in the first century. We need to be absolutely committed not just to knowing what the Bible teaches, but to living it. We need to be unreservedly given to doing life together, meeting formally as well as informally. We need to be persistent in our efforts to make Christ the center of that life together, making sure that we take full advantage of those formal and informal times to share communion, pray, and all the other things we can employ in the worship of Christ in our shared relationship with him.

Once we do these things, once we're fully devoted, that's when we'll start to see culture shift within the church, in contrast to the cultural shift we've seen in society around us. That's when others will see generosity, justice, freedom, compassion, joy, sincerity and all the other things they've been searching for in a culture that feels like it's run amok. That's when the church, Jesus' ecclesia, will enjoy favor with people who currently look at us with suspicion and rejection. That's when the Lord will add to our number daily those who are being saved. But if it was easy we'd probably already be doing it. And when we finally commit to that kind of life in Christ, in addition to finding favor with some people, we'll likely loose even more favor with others.

In chapter one of this book we see that Jesus gave the "keys of the kingdom" to his church. He appointed us as his stewards, responsible to carry out his wishes. Luke's brief description of that very first church is a powerful reminder that we are indeed Jesus' stewards. It's a responsibility we don't think of often, but it's a responsibility we dare not take lightly. It's a responsibility we must embrace fully.

Chapter Eight

Equipping People

So Christ himself gave the apostles, the prophets, the evangelists, the pastors and teachers, to equip his people for works of service, so that the body of Christ may be built up until we all reach unity in the faith and in the knowledge of the Son of God and become mature, attaining to the whole measure of the fullness of Christ.[121]

Last year I had the chance to attend a church that felt especially welcoming. I couldn't quite put my finger on what it was, but people seemed more open, more friendly, more relational somehow. The lobby was jammed with people talking, laughing, hugging and enjoying being together. The free coffee was right next to a fun little bookstore filled with inspirational posters and mugs. The worship was upbeat but not aggressive. The message was biblical but not pushy, focusing on God's love for me and for others. As the service ended people felt comfortable and loved – by the church and by God. It wasn't until later that I felt vaguely let down. Then it hit me: there was nothing in the experience that pushed me to be more. I was encouraged to be open to what God may or may not want to do in my life, but there was nothing about commitment to anything in particular. Nothing about making a difference in the world. Nothing about sacrifice and service. Nothing that suggested I could (or even should) be part of something larger than myself.

Sociologists call it Moralistic Therapeutic Deism. The idea is that there is a God, and that God wants us to be good and kind and fair to each other. This God wants us to feel good about ourselves and others. MTD is a trend first identified in a study of young people a number of years ago, but it's certainly not limited to young people. Reviewing the data, one scholar lamented:

The problem does not seem to be that churches are teaching young people badly, but that we are doing an exceedingly good job of teaching youth what we really believe: namely, that Christianity is not a big deal, that God requires little, and the church is a helpful social institution filled with nice people focused primarily on "folks like us"—which, of course, begs the question of whether we are really the church at all.[122]

Moralistic Therapeutic Deism isn't something churches have created on purpose over the past couple of decades. It's been a quiet evolution that's in part a reflection how the church has interacted with culture. As the church, we created systems and structures that made sense. Our leadership and organizational approach, our programming, our buildings and budgets were all developed in previous centuries. MTD is one of the outgrowths of the fact that those systems and structures did not readily adapt to the 21st century. I'm in no way suggesting that the way we do church is inherently wrong, or unbiblical. The church has had a tremendous impact on the world in the past few generations. It hasn't been perfect, but hundreds of millions of people from around the word will spend eternity together in the presence of God because he used us as well as those systems and structures. But we need to acknowledge that those same things that worked so well then, are now struggling with the shifts around us. Dallas Willard graciously says it this way: "We are on the verge of a time when the church is going to be able to make some decisions."[123] In truth, we are now in a time when we must make those decisions.

As we've already seen, Acts chapter two give us a description of what the very first church experience was like:

> They devoted themselves to the apostles' teaching and to fellowship, to the breaking of bread and to prayer. Everyone was filled with awe at the many wonders and signs performed by the apostles. All the believers were together and had everything in common. They sold property and possessions to give to anyone who had need. Every day they continued to meet together in the temple courts. They broke bread in their homes and ate together with glad and sincere hearts, praising God and enjoying the favor of all the people. And the Lord added to their number daily those who were being saved.[124]

When I consult with churches on their organizational development and structure, this is a passage that often forms the basis for discussion. Like a lot of the pastors I work with, I have historically missed two of the most critical take-aways. I've missed the fact that this is descriptive, not prescriptive. There's nothing in the passage that tells us we're supposed to do church the way they did; it's just a description of what they did. We should learn from that, but the Bible does not give us a specific model for how we are to "do" church. There's no place that clearly sets out a governance style. There's no place that tells us what kind of music to use. There's no place that describes how Sunday School should work; for that matter, Sunday School is not mentioned in the Bible at all. We're not even told whether our pastor should use expository or topical sermons. As we look at the New Testament, we see more differences than similarities in the way people did church. There are broad principles, but Jerusalem, Antioch, Ephesus, Corinth and all the others each did things a bit differently. That's important to keep in mind as we consider the best ways to equip people to be the church in the 21st century.

The second thing I usually read right by in this passage, more important for our discussion here: I miss the communal nature of this passage. It doesn't say "they each devoted themselves to the apostles' teaching." It says "they," plural, together, devoted themselves to the apostles' teaching. Look at the rest of those terms: they were "together," they had everything "in common." They continued to "meet together." They ate "together." This is not a passage that primarily tells us how to do church. This is a passage that describes what the Community of the Gospel looked like in the first century. They did life together, and they did ministry together. Interestingly, these days we struggle with both doing life and doing ministry together.

And don't miss verse 47. When they acted as community, they enjoyed the favor of all the people, and many of those people came to Christ. As the church in the 21st century, surely we want nothing less. As we strive to be the kind of community that enjoys the favor of people, and the kind of community that sees people come to Christ on a daily basis, we need to shift our attitudes and expectations in four key areas. We need to practice life together, we need to restructure our organization, we need to facilitate intergenerational discipleship, and we need to develop cultural awareness.

Practice Life Together

The early church in Jerusalem did life together. At least at the beginning of the church, they got together every day in the Temple courts. That's a lot of togetherness. This is not something we're very good at in the western world. We have remote controls for our garage door openers so we don't accidently encounter our neighbors as we get home from work. We have fences in our back yards so we can relax in privacy. We teach our kids not to talk to strangers. We see our church friends at church (which is why we call them "church friends"). Then we look forward to seeing them again next week. We do see some of them in our weekly Bible study, whenever something else doesn't get in the way. On the whole our church friends are for church. We have other friends for work, for our hobbies, and for other non-church settings. All of that means that we'll have to be more thoughtful and intentional in pursuing biblical community.

Probably the most pointed instruction for us along these lines is from Christ in John chapter 13: "A new command

I give you: Love one another. As I have loved you, so you must love one another. By this everyone will know that you are my disciples, if you love one another."[125] Much of what we hear in Christian teaching these days, related to the Moralistic Therapeutic Deism approach, talks about a generic love for everyone since God is love. It's true that God is love, and it's true that we're to love others. This command though is very specific, and very intense. The world won't know we are his disciples because we vaguely love everyone. The world will know we follow Christ because we sacrificially, demonstrably love each other. This is the kind of thing described in Acts chapter 2. This kind of brotherly love requires us to be part of each others' lives. It requires us to be together – a lot more than we're used to. It requires us to share with each other whenever we can meet each other's needs. It requires us to spend time studying and applying Scripture together. It requires us to think differently about what it means to be the church.

Restructure Our Organization

Much of what we think and what we do as followers of Christ is dictated by the way we have organized ourselves. For too long we have substituted content acquisition and positive emotion for the spiritual depth found in the Bible. We have allowed American individualism to isolate us from true ecclesia, to the point that we're not even sure we want ecclesia. And as we've noted earlier, we have begun to think of the church as the programs and pastors, systems and structures. In other words, we have created a mental model of church that has replaced the people with the organization. Peter Block, in his insightful work on the nature of community and belonging, reminds us that "...transformation hinges on changing the structure of how we engage each other."[126] If we have any hope of being the church we need to be in the 21st century, one of the first places we need to look is at that organizational structure. The reality is that most of the way we do church evolved in a previous era. And it worked well. Think back to our discussion of shifting generations and recall that our society used to place a high value on hierarchy and institutional loyalty. It made sense for our churches to include staff and leadership hierarchies as we did. It made sense for our ministries to assume people would naturally submit to leadership, and that institutional loyalty would lead to long tenures and high volunteerism.

Then culture shifted. And churches across the country find themselves struggling to maintain programs that used to be no-brainers. Children's Sunday School is a prime example. Over the past decade or so volunteerism in kids' ministry has become a growing problem. There simply aren't enough people willing to spend an hour with kids on a Sunday morning. And those that are willing to help are no longer interested in serving every week. As a result, churches have unwittingly begun to feed on themselves in order to maintain Sunday School and other programs. The unexamined thinking goes something like this: Sunday School is vitally important for both children's discipleship and church growth; therefore we need to grow the church so that we'll have enough people to maintain our kids ministry; which in turn grows the Sunday School; so we need to grow the church ... and the cycle continues. Quietly the focus moves away from drawing people to Christ and toward drawing people to the church.

The church staff grows proportionately larger to compensate. This then ramps up the emphasis on hierarchy as increasing amounts of ministry is done by paid staff. The staff becomes overloaded when people expect too much of them, so we hire more staff to help with the load. People see the large staff and assume the staff can handle the work of ministry so they volunteer less and expect more. Which increases the load on the staff. You see where this is going.

We've already seen that it's not only the professionals, the pastors, who are described as priests in the New Testament. That passage in 1st Peter is clear: we are all part of that "royal priesthood," with all the privileges and responsibilities that go with the priesthood. Pastors have a unique position in the church, but it has more to do with the privilege we pastors have to do this full time than with anything else. The uniqueness of the pastoral position is decidedly not to do the work of ministry as we normally think of it. The Apostle Paul speaks to that very thing:

> So Christ himself gave the apostles, the prophets, the evangelists, the pastors and teachers, to equip his people for works of service, so that the body of Christ may be built up until we all reach unity in the faith and in the knowledge of the Son of God and become

mature, attaining to the whole measure of the fullness of Christ.[127]

Normally when we talk about spiritual gifts we rightly think of the gifts that each believer has been given through the power of the Holy Spirit. These gifts are designed to draw people to Christ and build up the church, the Community of the Gospel. In this particular passage Paul adds a side note to his definition of spiritual gifts. Some people with these specific gifts (apostles, prophets, evangelists, pastors and teachers) are in turn Christ's gift to the church. Not so they can do the work for the rest of us, but very clearly in order to equip God's people so God's people can do the work they're called and gifted to do. "So that the body of Christ [the church] may be built up … until we become mature." Jesus' people need to be doing those "works of service;" it's part of God's design for us to reach unity and maturity. In other words, as long as the pastors are busy doing the work of ministry, they're not busy equipping people to do the work of ministry, and the body of Christ will not be built up as it's supposed to be. And we will not attain "to the whole measure of the fullness of Christ." Now that's sobering.

Equipping people for their works of service makes sense in our heads, but we don't always do it. Here's one example. It's one of those examples that might be a little sensitive. Please know that it's not intended as criticism so much as it is something to make us go "hmmm." Don't answer this out loud (unless the people around you are already used to that kind of thing): if you find yourself in the hospital, who do you think should come visit you? If you've spent lots of time hanging around traditional churches, the answer is "Why, the pastor of course." Here's the next question: "why?" The first answer for most of us churchy people is something like: "Well, because that's what pastors do." Push a little more and the answer is "Because it's their job." Please understand, I'm not suggesting that pastors should not visit people in the hospital. I'm just drawing our attention to the way we've designed the organization. Is it really his job? Not according to Paul. We just read that the pastor's job is to equip people for works of service, not to do it for them. When I push that one more time I'll get the response: "But the pastor is the one who knows how to visit people." If anything, that's even more disconcerting. Why is it that the pastor is the only one who knows how to make hospital visits? Those of us who are pastors need to consider why we're the ones making those hospital visits. Sometimes it's totally appropriate for us, as members of the church, to visit friends and others who are hurting. More often though, we assume that because we're pastors we're the best ones to do it. Sometimes, lots of times probably, we're doing people a disservice by taking on that kind of responsibility. And it's often out of our own arrogance: "Well, I am the qualified one as you know. Can't leave an important ministry like this to just anyone." And those who aren't pastors may want to consider why you expect your pastor to do that kind of thing. That's not what his primary job is supposed to be. Consider this: every hour your pastor spends visiting people in the hospital is an hour he's not equipping someone else. That in turn makes it less likely that the body of Christ will become truly mature.

All of this together means that we have somehow created a system in which people serve the organization rather than having an organization that serves the people. We've become more concerned with finding people to be Sunday School teachers than we are with what happens in the classrooms. We've become more concerned with filling the ranks of our ushers and deacons than we are with whether we're extending biblical hospitality through those people. We need to revisit the systems and structures, programs and policies that have gradually grown and quietly become sacred. Each local body needs to assess why it does what it does, and consider which of those things are in place because they've "always been there" and which of those things are effectively supporting the Community of the Gospel, equipping people, and drawing attention to the person and work of Christ.

Now that I've thoroughly messed with your head by suggesting that some of the most pastoral things your pastor does might not actually be the best thing for the church, and that children's Sunday School might need to be reconsidered, let's move along.

Facilitate Intergenerational Discipleship

Most of us are well aware of Jesus' mandate to his followers from Matthew 28:

> Then Jesus came to them and said, "All authority in heaven and on earth has been given to me. Therefore

go and make disciples of all nations, baptizing them in the name of the Father and of the Son and of the Holy Spirit, and teaching them to obey everything I have commanded you. And surely I am with you always, to the very end of the age."[128]

"Go make disciples." So that we're all on the same page, I'm just using a very simple definition of disciple here. A disciple is one who follows Jesus. "Go help people follow Jesus." It's clear, it's compelling, and we commit a lot of our time and energy and money toward it. There are actually two parts to the command, both of which have generated huge amounts of scholarly writing and discussion. We're going to bypass the nuances here and stick with the straightforward stuff. Scholars can debate the mode, meaning, timing and everything else about baptism, but for us the focus is on the fact that baptism in this passage is an indication that a person is following Christ. That's the first part of this command, and it ties into Peter's discussion of living and proclaiming the Gospel. We need to be sharing Christ in such a way that people follow Jesus. In our next chapter we'll spend some time talking about what it looks like to engage the society around us. For now, we want to look more closely at the second part of this command: "Teaching them to obey everything I have commanded you." When we talk about "discipleship" that's usually the part we're talking about.

Think for a minute about your own church. What does its discipleship program look like? Some of us use different words, and there are some creative twists, but most of us naturally think about our Christian Education programs, primarily Sunday School and Bible Studies. Most of our discipleship revolves around a Sunday School model that began in the late 1700's. By the mid 1900's it had developed into something that looks pretty much like what we do today. Now think about the words we've used to describe what we do: Christian "Education," Sunday "School" and Bible "Study." Hold that thought for a minute. If you went to church as a kid, you almost assuredly attended Sunday School, even if your childhood memories are a little vague about the whole thing. If you continued going to church into adulthood, you very likely taught a Sunday School class as one time or another. So even if it isn't your favorite memory, you know as well as I do that those Christian Education programs for children, youth and adults have been highly successful for a lot of years.

Recall some of the things we know about 21st century culture. We know that the cultural bell curve is pulling people away from the institutional church. We know that many of the next generation switch jobs every three years. We know that traditional learning mechanisms have been replaced with the internet and social media. We know that people value experience over proposition. We know that people are skeptical of just about any institution, but they're open to relationships.

Now compare what we know of American culture with the way we approach discipleship. As the world shifts, our primary model of discipleship needs to shift with it. There's definitely a place for Bible study and teaching, but we have to remember that the primary point of Jesus' command wasn't content acquisition. He didn't say "teach them everything I have commanded you." He said,

"teach them to obey everything I have commanded you."
His point was not to see how much we could learn, but to
see how much like him we could become. He said, "The
student is not above the teacher, but everyone who is
fully trained will be like their teacher."[129]

The test of a mature disciple is not whether they know
everything their teacher knows. The test is whether they
are like their teacher. We need to start thinking about
how best to come alongside people as they journey
toward Christ, and toward becoming more like him. In a
culture that highly values authentic relationships, I
suggest that we need to become more relational in our
discipleship. We also need to be more intentionally
intergenerational.

Consider current research which has overwhelmingly
shown that "Young adults who continue their
involvement in a local church beyond their teen years are
twice as likely as those who don't to have a close
personal friendship with an older adult in their faith
community (59% vs. 31% among church dropouts).
They're also twice as likely to have had a mentor other
than a pastor or youth minister (28% vs. 11%)."[130] There
is a profound correlation between lasting faith and close,
personal relationships among young people and older
mentors. And the research shows that those older
mentors are men and women other than pastors and
parents. That doesn't displace parents by any stretch of
the imagination. The Barna Group says that "The best
data across disciplines confirms that parents still carry
the most important weight in their kids' faith
development. ... This means the role of ministry leaders

who care about kids must also include the care, equipping, and formation of parents and families."[131] So while parents are still the primary champions of spiritual growth in kids, and while we need to equip parents for their role, we absolutely must find ways to involve other adults in our kids' lives.

It's not that we should never break up into age groups, but if our primary model of discipleship is all about age groups, not only do we break with research, more importantly we miss some key directives in the Bible. The writer of Psalm 71 begged God to give him time to disciple the next generation: "Even when I am old and gray, do not forsake me, my God, till I declare your power to the next generation, your mighty acts to all who are to come."[132] Another Psalm says it this way: "One generation commends your works to another; they tell of your mighty acts."[133] Paul makes kind of a big deal about it with Titus:

Teach the older men to be temperate, worthy of respect, self-controlled, and sound in faith, in love and in endurance. Likewise, teach the older women to be reverent in the way they live, not to be slanderers or addicted to much wine, but to teach what is good. Then they can urge the younger women to love their husbands and children,[134]

These and many other passages place a high level of responsibility on those of us who are older. We don't get to wait until young people come ask us to regale them with stories about how things were back in the day. Notice the action words: we are to "declare God's power to the next generation." We are to "tell of his mighty acts" one generation to another. We are to "teach what is good" to younger men and women. We need to take the initiative to enter into authentic relationships with the next generation, doing life with them in a way that allows them to both see and hear about Christ. We need to do life with them in a way that helps them move closer and closer to maturity in Him.

As a pastor I talk to way too many older Christians whose attitude is: "I've put my time in. Let the younger folks take over. They have more energy anyway." Paul and Peter were both in their 60s and actively leading when they were executed. Daniel was in his 80s when he was thrown in the lions' den. John was in his 90s when he died, still going strong. Our responsibilities shift as we get older, but they also get weightier. And to be honest, this whole thing about authentic relationships is every bit as hard as it sounds. Given the massive cultural shifts over the past decade, intergenerational conversations aren't easy. And I don't know about you, but I've never gotten over the dual fear of rejection and inadequacy. What if I reach out to someone and he doesn't want me in his life? What if I get into a discipling relationship and I don't know what to say? How would I even relate to someone who thinks so differently than I do? And how do I even start? What, do I walk up to someone and say, "you don't know me, but you seem young and I'd like to develop an authentic relationship with you in which I show you how to be more like Jesus?"

Here's what I've learned from personal experience. First, simply ask someone to have a cup of coffee with you. If you really want to sound like you're young at heart, suggest bubble tea instead of coffee. I usually say something like this: "I've been watching the news lately and realized that I don't see the world the way younger folks do. I've been really impressed with our short conversations and I'd love to buy you a cup of coffee and get your take on what's happening in the world right now." I have never had someone turn me down when I asked for their opinion.

Second, this doesn't work if your primary point in having coffee is to set that next generation straight. Partly, that's not authentic at all and they'll see right through you. Partly, you're not going to be able to speak into someone's life if you don't understand them. Authentic, relational discipleship begins with a whole lot of questions. Just listen. Ask for clarification. Be nonjudgmental. And be patient: relationships take a while to develop; trust takes even longer.

This biblical mandate to practice intergenerational discipleship needs to be an extension of the conversation we started in the previous section about restructuring the way we organize ourselves. In what ways might your church restructure itself to facilitate discipleship that is more geared toward life transformation than it is toward content acquisition? What can you do to lower some of the walls that arise when people become more concerned with personal preferences than they are with "attaining the whole measure of the fullness of Christ?" In what ways might your church encourage intergenerational discipleship as more significant than age graded classes and demographically similar groups?

If not your whole church, how might you begin to make that shift within your own sphere of influence?

Develop Cultural Awareness

One of the positive side effects of intergenerational discipleship is likely to be a greater cultural awareness and sensitivity among the church. That won't always be the case, but cultural shifts, especially in the church, are more pronounced in younger generations. As those of us who are chronologically more advanced spend time in meaningful, humble relationships, we'll gain a deeper understanding of the times we live in.

If God's people sequester themselves in our so-called "holy huddles" we will never understand enough about our world and our immediate culture. We will be ineffective in our efforts to engage others with the amazing truth of the person of Christ. We live in a culture that values justice, but is completely unaware that God is the God of true justice. We live in a culture that desperately searches for authenticity, but is completely unaware that true authenticity is only found in Jesus. We live in a culture deeply concerned over issues of ecology, but is completely unaware of how deeply God is concerned for his creation. Unfortunately, we hang out in churches that are only vaguely aware of God's place in all these issues, much less are they aware of what the body of Christ should be and what it should do in the 21st century.

As the church in the 21st century places a strong emphasis on preaching the unadulterated, undiluted truths of Scripture, we must do so with an eye toward what it means to be Community of the Gospel, and how we live and proclaim that Gospel. Preaching, as well as other teaching, needs to include passages and topics which are clearly pertinent to the issues people are worried about and talking about as soon as they leave the confines of a church building. What does the Bible say about justice? What does it say about stewarding God's creation? Or about gender? Or racism? Sexual norms?

The challenge for the church in the 21st century will be to stop fighting against the cultural shift (we've already lost that fight) and embrace the opportunities the new paradigm presents. It's sad that most churches inadvertently avoid those opportunities when they go about business as usual. Many a pastor is loath to tackle difficult topics for fear of offending someone, or for fear of losing someone's financial support. Worse, if indeed it gets worse, is the rationale that tackling challenging issues will force the church to take an unpopular position, thereby losing its good standing in the community.

And so we pastors leave aside Paul's instruction to equip God's people and focus instead on encouraging God's people. Ultimately, that leaves God's people feeling good about themselves, about God and about their pastor, but ill equipped to deal with the world outside their church walls. The truth is, we can teach biblical truth without taking formal political stands. Biblical truth is not the same as conservative (or progressive) worldviews.

If we're to deal with issues specific to our own local context, we'll need to diligently pursue an understanding of what those issues are. Is your community dealing with poverty? Immigration? Education? Racism? Drug abuse? Mental health? No one church can deal with everything, but we must all deal with something. As we identify key issues we'll quickly discover the very things people are most interested in. We'll discover those things they are most in need of understanding from a biblical perspective. The trick for most churches, of course, will be to focus on equipping people to be the Community of the Gospel rather than starting another program they're supposed to volunteer for. Imagine the transformation in our lives and communities if we stopped centralizing everything within the confines of the institution.

As we've already seen, Peter has lots to say about the church and what it means to be the church. And he is deeply aware that being a Community of the Gospel which lives and proclaims the Gospel means we need to present it in a way that is meaningful to the culture we live in. At one point he said, "But in your hearts revere Christ as Lord. Always be prepared to give an answer to everyone who asks you to give the reason for the hope that you have. But do this with gentleness and respect."[135] In the context of equipping the church, this means we'll need to prepare people for their inevitable encounters with culture. As Christ-followers we need to understand enough about culture to competently give the reason for the hope that we have. Let's face it, even those who are fully immersed in culture don't generally take the time to understand it.

Paul gives us a great example with his encounters in Athens. The story is told in Acts chapter 17.

> While Paul was waiting for them in Athens, he was greatly distressed to see that the city was full of idols. So he reasoned in the synagogue with both Jews and God-fearing Greeks, as well as in the marketplace day by day with those who happened to be there. A group of Epicurean and Stoic philosophers began to debate with him. Some of them asked, "What is this babbler trying to say?" Others remarked, "He seems to be advocating foreign gods." They said this because Paul was preaching the good news about Jesus and the resurrection. Then they took him and brought him to a meeting of the Areopagus, where they said to him, "May we know what this new teaching is that you are presenting? You are bringing some strange ideas to our ears, and we would like to know what they mean." (All the Athenians and the foreigners who lived there spent their time doing nothing but talking about and listening to the latest ideas.) Paul then stood up in the meeting of the Areopagus and said: "People of Athens! I see that in every way you are very religious. For as I walked around and looked carefully at your objects of worship, I even found an altar with this inscription: to an unknown god. So you are ignorant of the very thing you worship—and this is what I am going to proclaim to you.[136]

Paul is waiting for his friends when he starts to pay attention to the culture of Athens. It's a culture not unlike our own. As Paul discovers, people consider themselves very spiritual and love talking about spiritual sounding things. They are so open that they've even built an altar to "The Unknown God." Now that's politically correct: making a place for the worship of a god they'd never heard of just to make sure he wasn't offended in case he existed. Paul is paying close attention and has a keen understanding of the world he lives in. So as people start asking questions he's able to use the culture of the Athenians as a starting point for talking about God. In the discussion that ensues, he quotes two different Greek poets to make his point. In his first century context, that's much the same as if he'd quoted something from Ariana Grande in our day. Paul intentionally develops his cultural awareness, noting that "I have become all things to all people so that by all possible means I might save some. I do all this for the sake of the gospel."[137]

All that (understanding culture and becoming all things to all people) is not to say that we agree with, or become like, the culture we are living among. Our culture, for example, places a tremendous value on individualism and autonomy. Ecclesia declares that we are not simply a collection of individuals. Rather we belong to each other. We can understand what culture believes about individualism without embracing the same value. Like the men of Issachar, we do this so that in understanding the times, we will know how to respond. We do this so that like Paul we are able to find points of connection with the people we encounter. And like Paul we do it for the sake of the Gospel.

It's the Little Things

It's not always easy to start thinking about the church differently. Those of us who've been part of the church for decades don't know anything different. And what we do know just seems wrong. Where would we even begin to address some of the things we've talked about in this book? You probably have at least some of your own ideas and that's likely the best place to start since you know your church and your context. But just to give you additional food for thought, or perhaps just to jump start your thought process, here are a few quick suggestions.

Biblical Preaching. We noted at the beginning of this chapter that one of the prevalent concerns in the church right now is preaching that inadvertently espouses Moralistic Therapeutic Deism. The idea (so you don't have to go back and look) is that there is a God, who wants us to be good and kind and fair to each other, and wants us to feel good about ourselves and others. Part of the problem of course is that the truth of that idea obscures the fact that as good as it is to be encouraging, MTD preaching does nothing to fulfill our primary responsibility as pastors. Our real job is to equip people. Since the weekend pulpit is the primary place for most of our teaching, that's also the logical place for much of our equipping. I am not advocating a specific style of preaching (say, exegetical over-against topical) but whatever style is best in a particular context, preaching must be unequivocally based on the clear teaching of the Bible. "Feel good" messages accomplish exactly what they set out to accomplish: they make people feel good about themselves while the message is fresh in their minds. But the feeling fades.

I'm also not suggesting that we need to be offensive to new believers or those who don't yet follow Christ; or that we should preach hellfire and brimstone every weekend. I am suggesting though, that the church, the people, the Community of the Gospel, needs more than we're giving them. Especially with the massive cultural shift around us, people need to know how to respond to that culture. We need to be talking about social and individual justice issues. We need to be looking to see what Scripture says about gender issues, racism and the abuse of power. We need to consider the church's response to environmental concerns; most of the church doesn't even realize that God's mandate for us to steward the earth has never been revoked. The Bible speaks to all of these issues and we are remiss when we don't preach those passages.

Biblical Worldview. As we emphasize biblical preaching, including the discussion of issues most significant to people struggling to live in a culture that's lost its bearing, we're helping them develop a biblical worldview. "A worldview is a set of fundamental beliefs that inform the way we see and engage the world."[138] We need to intentionally set about cultivating a worldview founded on the Gospel. This includes a watchfulness over both the quality and quantity of that which we allow to influence us individually and collectively. The Apostle cautions us to think on those things that are true, noble, right and pure.[139] We must ensure that the things which influence us, the things which we allow into our lives, are only those things that support the improvement of our lives and worldview. Ed Stetzer comments: "Paul connects the quality of our influences to the quality of our spiritual lives, which is why we must think through how we are shaped by the people, media, and activities we experience."[140] Newer to the church's discussion of those things which influence our lives is the issue of quantity. Even those things which are positive, if perhaps somewhat inane, can be problematic if consumed in too large a quantity. The word "binging" comes to mind. I first discovered the wonderful world of binging from my own high school children. My family subscribes to Netflix and we each have our own devices which link to the account. That allows us to watch as much as we want of whatever we want whenever we want to watch it. I've learned from personal experience how difficult it is to think on things that are pure and noble when you're spending several hours a day on that which is inane, mediocre and frivolous. Of course, if the church isn't helping us develop a biblically informed worldview, who's to say what's inane, mediocre and frivolous? And once I'm steeped in everything Netflix has to offer, who's to say which values and cultural norms are pure and noble and true?

Sharing Faith. We know that the cultural bell curve has shifted away from Christianity and into secularism. We know that what once pulled people to church and the things of the church no longer function as they once did. At the same time, we know that people are still lost and hurting. In the first century Jesus said, "Don't you have a saying, 'It's still four months until harvest'? I tell you, open your eyes and look at the fields! They are ripe for harvest."[141] That is still true in the 21st century. Culture has changed and priorities have shifted, but God is still working in hearts, drawing people to Jesus. As followers of Christ, we need to be prepared to boldly, clearly, and simply proclaim the Gospel. Too many local churches relegate faith sharing to exceptional evangelists, and reserve equipping to special classes for those who are brave enough to attend. We need to move evangelism out of our church basements and into the limelight. We need to celebrate those with the spiritual gift of evangelism (as we should celebrate all the gifts), but we need to remove the notion that boldly sharing faith is exceptional. Sharing faith must become normative, and all the more so as culture pulls people away from settings where they might hear of Christ.

Rejection. Paul makes it clear that when the church is truly being the church, when it is living as the Community of the Gospel, proclaiming and living that Gospel clearly and boldly, we will not generally encounter what we think of as success. Our churches may not grow, our co-workers may not center their lives on Jesus, and our lives may not be filled with accolades from family and friends. Rather he likens our proclamation to an aroma that is pleasing to God and the church, but a stench to others:

> But thanks be to God, who always leads us as captives in Christ's triumphal procession and uses us to spread the aroma of the knowledge of him everywhere. For we are to God the pleasing aroma of Christ among those who are being saved and those who are perishing. To the one we are an aroma that

brings death; to the other, an aroma that brings life. And who is equal to such a task?[142]

Part of equipping the church to represent Christ in the 21st century is to equip people to face rejection as well as acceptance.

Equipping the church to be the Community of the Gospel in the 21st century is not for the faint of heart. It requires thought and effort. It requires prayer and deliberation. Frighteningly, it requires change. I was in a prayer meeting not that long ago when one of the beautiful members of the group thanked God for the wonderful church she was part of and ended with: "Please keep it as it is." The sentiment behind the prayer was heartfelt: it was a good group of people who truly loved Jesus and loved each other. If you didn't know better, you'd swear it was a wonderful example of ecclesia in action. But behind the prayer was fear; fear that someone new might want to join and mess everything up; fear that something might shake up the status quo; fear of change. Truth be told, like many of us, she joined the group for what it was, not for what it could (or perhaps should) be.

We cannot continue to do what we've been doing and expect anything to be different. We embrace change – as long as it's someone else doing the changing. As Chris Nye observed "God has not given us a first century church to preserve, but a 21st century church to lead."[143] Neil Cole said much the same thing: "We must realize that the church of the past is not equipped for the opportunities of the future. We must shift in our systemic core so that we can take advantage of the global opportunities we face."[144] We need to stop looking at the obstacles and start taking advantages of the opportunities.

Chapter Nine

Engaging Society

See, I am doing a new thing! Now it springs up; do you not perceive it? I am making a way in the wilderness and streams in the wasteland.[145]

A year ago I somewhat reluctantly agreed to chair a non-profit organization dedicated to preventing mental health and drug abuse problems among youth in our county. I say "reluctantly" because I was concerned about my time commitment. The county I live in has rates of youth drug abuse, depression, anxiety and suicide much higher than the national average, so the organization is sorely needed. This new organization is really designed to be a coalition of other groups and programs, all sharing the same concern about our youth. Right now there are over 60 different organizations representing a wide range of values and philosophies. Every school district in the county, the police departments, the health department, private counselors, city and county governments, and a host of other non-profits are working together to transform the youth culture of our county. It's exhilarating to watch high levels of participation in our meetings, to read the dozens of emails that fly back and forth between organizations that would otherwise be functioning in their silos, and to be part of professional and lay training events associated with what we do.

At one of our recent meetings our coordinator was leading part of the meeting and reminded the participants that "we're working to create a culture of caring." Watching heads nod in agreement throughout the room was energizing. And then I looked a little more closely. And I realized how little representation there was from the church. Among the 60 or so organizations involved, only two were Christian organizations. Two more of the leaders in the room were believers. In an organization working to create a culture of caring, where is the church?

In our meetings we talk about ways our schools and municipalities can be doing more to help kids with moral and other healthy life choices. The church is not part of those conversations. Another major topic of conversation is how best we can help engage parents so they can better support their kids. One of the major concerns is finding "safe spaces" where the parents would be willing come for training. Disappointingly, church is not even mentioned as a place people might feel comfortable. As a tangent to that conversation, someone suggested that older parents might be able to mentor newer parents. Once again, the church is not part of that conversation.

I've gone out of my way as a pastor to invite other Christian organizations. They just don't see their role in a secular nonprofit. One said they were too busy. I can't decide whether to be frustrated or optimistic. I'm optimistic that our county is talking about the kinds of things the church cares about too. Who isn't concerned with youth depression and drug use? And the solutions often suggested are phenomenal opportunities for the church. Need a safe place to meet? There are plenty of church facilities that are largely empty on weeknights. Need older parents to mentor newer parents? Sounds a lot like intergenerational discipleship to me. I'm frustrated that the church is busy doing its own thing and doesn't have time or inclination to be part of its own community.

As I look around the room in those meetings, it's a good reminder of some of the things we've already learned about 21st century culture. Notably, people simply aren't interested – church isn't even part of the conversation among the coalition members. On the rare occasion Christianity is mentioned, it's not mentioned in a positive way. One of the major challenges we face as the church in America is the growing negative perception of church in our society. A recent Barna report noted that among the unchurched "… almost half (49%) could not identify a single favorable impact of the Christian community …"[146] In other words, many of what the church believes to be positive contributions to the world around us go completely unnoticed by the unchurched.

As I work with this community group, I'm regularly faced with the reality that being a pastor is a major strike against me. The people I work with are kind, caring and passionate about helping people. They treat me with respect and appreciate my contribution. But in many ways they seem slightly confused as to why I'm there. It's simply not what pastors and churches do. As we've seen already, church is viewed as part of the problem rather than part of the solution. At first I found this somewhat offensive. Don't they appreciate all the work my church is doing around the world? Don't they know how much money we pour into relief and development work in our own community as well as other countries? Aren't they pleased with hundreds of hours of free counseling we provide to anyone who needs it? Don't they enjoy the fact that people who are part of our church give their time and money to dozens of local charities and non-profits?

When I stop my internal tirade long enough to reflect more rationally, I realize the answer is "No." As it turns out, they don't appreciate all the time, money and effort my church pours into work around the world. How can they? They aren't part of my church and have no idea what we do. Even if they do become aware of it, they aren't followers of Christ and can't appreciate our efforts to live and proclaim the Gospel. Besides, I realize, it isn't supposed to be about my church anyway. Christ is at the center, not my church. And Jesus never calls us to bring people to church. He calls us to go to them.

The last words Matthew records are a command from Jesus to his followers:

> Then Jesus came to them and said, "All authority in heaven and on earth has been given to me. Therefore go and make disciples of all nations, baptizing them in the name of the Father and of the Son and of the Holy Spirit, and teaching them to obey everything I have commanded you. And surely I am with you always, to the very end of the age."[147]

"Go and make disciples." Not "make every effort to attract people." Mark ends his gospel with the same command: "He said to them, 'Go into all the world and preach the gospel to all creation.'"[148] It's not a command limited to a few select missionaries. Jesus' last words to his followers were to go. John's gospel says the same thing, this time with a pleasant twist: "Again Jesus said, 'Peace be with you! As the Father has sent me, I am sending you.'"[149]

When Jesus makes these statements, it's not long after his death. His followers are understandably afraid. They're huddled in a locked room, hiding from the same Jewish leaders who promoted Jesus' crucifixion. Jesus shows up in the middle of the locked room and tells them to be at peace. I tend to read right by that little word, as if it's a generic greeting. It might have been a generic greeting, had things been different. But the disciples are terrified. They're hiding from the same leaders who had killed (cruelly killed) the man they have put their faith in. To be told by Jesus himself to be at peace is no generic greeting in these circumstances.

But it isn't a message of safety. Jesus doesn't tell them to be at peace because he guarantees no Jewish leader will find them. He tells them to be at peace because the Holy Spirit will come to them. At which point they are to go make disciples. They are to go into all the world (including the scary streets of Jerusalem). They are not being called to gather; they are being sent: "As the Father has sent me, I am sending you." Sent into a world that does not appreciate all they will do. Sent into a world that is not particularly interested in the Gospel. Sent into a world that would rather worship false gods than the one true God.

The command of Jesus is not limited to a few frightened disciples in the first century. It is a command for all of his followers, including those of us in the 21st century. We are instructed to go. We are instructed to engage the society we live in with the transformative power of the Gospel. As usual, Jesus himself provides the example of what that looks like.

Now he had to go through Samaria. So he came to a town in Samaria called Sychar, near the plot of ground Jacob had given to his son Joseph. Jacob's well was there, and Jesus, tired as he was from the journey, sat down by the well. It was about noon. When a Samaritan woman came to draw water, Jesus said to her, "Will you give me a drink?" (His disciples had gone into the town to buy food.) The Samaritan woman said to him, "You are a Jew and I am a Samaritan woman. How can you ask me for a drink?" (For Jews do not associate with Samaritans.) Jesus answered her, "If you knew the gift of God and who it is that asks you for a drink, you would have asked him and he would have given you living water." "Sir," the woman said, "you have nothing to draw with and the well is deep. Where can you get this living water? Are you greater than our father Jacob, who gave us the well and drank from it himself, as did also his sons and his livestock?" Jesus answered, "Everyone who drinks this water will be thirsty again, but whoever drinks the water I give them will never thirst. Indeed, the water I give them will become in them a spring of water welling up to eternal life." The woman said to him, "Sir, give me this water so that I won't get thirsty and have to keep coming here to draw water." He told her, "Go, call your husband and come back." "I have no husband," she replied. Jesus said to her, "You are right when you say you have no husband. The fact is, you have had five husbands, and the man you now have is not your husband. What you have just said is quite true." "Sir," the woman said, "I can see that you are a prophet. Our ancestors worshiped on this mountain, but you Jews claim that the place where we must worship is in Jerusalem." "Woman," Jesus replied, "believe me, a time is coming when you will worship the Father neither on this mountain nor in Jerusalem. You Samaritans worship what you do not know; we worship what we do know, for salvation is from the Jews. Yet a time is coming and has now come when the true worshipers will worship the Father in the Spirit and in truth, for they are the kind of worshipers the Father seeks. God is spirit, and his worshipers must worship in the Spirit and in truth." The woman said, "I know that Messiah" (called Christ) "is coming. When he comes, he will explain everything to us." Then Jesus declared, "I, the one speaking to you—I am he."[150]

There's so much depth and nuance in this story! In order to get to our point, we'll just skim the highlights. Jesus and his disciples are walking from Judea to Galilee, trying to keep a relatively low profile in Israel. Technically, they didn't "have" to go through Samaria, they could have walked around. In fact, in the first century Jews normally walk many, many miles out of their way to avoid Samaria. At this point in history the Jews and the Samaritans aren't exactly on speaking terms. Among many cultural differences, they have some strong differences of opinion about religion. Jesus had to go through Samaria in order to have this unusual encounter at the well, not because there wasn't another way to travel. The whole thing gets stranger as the story progresses.

It's bad enough that they're actually in Samaria, then Jesus initiates conversation with a woman. He even has the temerity to ask for a cup of water. Normally, a Jewish man would not have been traveling through Samaria. He would not have initiated conversation with a woman. And he most certainly would not have used her cup to drink; on top of everything else that would have made him ritually unclean. The woman is obviously surprised but does as Jesus requests. Jesus continues the conversation, moving from strange to shocking as he guides the chat from the idea of well-water all the way to the conclusion that he was the Messiah, the one around whom she could center her life.

A little while later his disciples rejoin him and have a similarly unusual conversation. While that conversation is going on, the woman has gone back to town and let everyone know what happened. "Many of the Samaritans from that town believed in him."[151] As I said, this is such a rich story and we're only skimming the surface. We're looking at this story here to see how Jesus models what he expects from us. His disciples would surely have remembered this bizarre experience when later he told them to go and make disciples. There are five basic principles to follow as we seek to live out Jesus' command and follow his example: Reclaim, Reflect, Remember, Relearn, and Relate.

Reclaim: Live As Ecclesia

While these five principles aren't really sequential, if there was a first one it would be to reclaim what it means to live as Jesus' ecclesia. As Jesus chats with the Samaritan woman, he makes one of several unusual statements: "Yet a time is coming and has now come when the true worshipers will worship the Father in the Spirit and in truth, for they are the kind of worshipers the Father seeks." Even as Jesus talks about spirit and truth, one of the significant differences between the Jews and Samaritans is the correct location for worship. Like we tend to do, the Jews in the first century have replaced the idea of being God's people with the institution of religion. For them it's all about going to the Temple and observing the law. They don't think much about what it means to live as God's people. For us it's all about going to church and we don't think much about being the church. As we've seen many times in this book, Jesus' ecclesia is not the institution, it's the people. Sitting at the well, Jesus is correcting the woman's understanding of what it means to follow him. He's helping her (and us) see that it's not about the institution of religion. Church isn't the Temple or the church building. It's not the systems and the laws. It's not about the Pharisees or the pastors. Church is the Community of the Gospel. We've already talked a lot about that in this book, so I'll just remind us that if we're going to follow Jesus' command to go and make disciples, we need to reclaim what it means to be Jesus' ecclesia.

Reflect: Examine Our Assumptions

As we've already seen, a tremendous amount of the way we go about doing church is based on a different culture. We need to take a hard look at what we do and why we do it. We need to go back to Scripture with an eye toward critiquing our assumptions. We need to be willing to make difficult changes when we find ourselves holding as sacred things Scripture does not hold sacred. Jesus' conversation with the Samaritan woman challenges her assumptions as well as those of the disciples. The woman asks "You are a Jew and I am a Samaritan woman. How can you ask me for a drink?" The disciples are "surprised to find him talking with a woman."[152] It's never occurred to any of them that there's another, even a better, way to understand the world around them. Everything they assume about what is culturally right and wrong is turned upside down in one encounter at a well in Samaria.

Like the Jews and Samaritans in the first century we take what we do for granted. We rarely stop long enough to reflect on "why" we do it. As a very simple example, we know how bulletins ought to look, so that's the way they look. What if we didn't use bulletins? What would happen then? Should we make a decision like that based on our expectation that some people would be upset if we didn't give them a packet of paper when they entered the worship center? What if we used an app instead? There's a lot of affordable options out there. It would save paper. And photocopying. People could give right on their phones. They could follow the sermon outline and even take notes. I was visiting a church this past weekend and did just that. Easy to download, easy to use. But then what about the people who don't use apps? Keep examining our assumptions. How many people don't use apps? Is that the primary group we're trying to speak to? If so, might there be a better way to handle bulletins? Or, after we've truly examined what we're doing and why we're doing it, should we keep doing exactly what we've been doing?

What about Sunday School? What are we trying to accomplish with that program? Given the times we live in, is a traditional age-graded children's Sunday School program the best way to accomplish our aims? If our church is like so many others that can't seem to find enough volunteers to run the program effectively, should we be doing something else? Or should we reevaluate the way we challenge people to volunteer? Or is there something else altogether we should be considering?

What about the way we handle benevolence? What about our expectations of our pastoral staff? Are we involved in the right mission projects? How are we present in the community? Are we equipping people in a way that makes sense in the 21st century? Or just in the 20th century? Are we creating structures and systems that facilitate ecclesia? Or are we holding on to things that are more likely to distract or even discourage ecclesia? My point here is not that we need to jettison everything we've held dear for many, many years. My point is that culture has shifted around us and we cannot afford to take things for granted.

In addition to reflecting on our assumptions regarding the church, we need to examine our expectations about people outside the church. Think back to the pizza restaurant analogy. We've long assumed that people would love to come try our pizza. Who doesn't like pizza? We just need to make sure we have the best pizza in town and people will flock to our restaurant. Won't they? That used to be true. And for many of us, it's hard to imagine that pizza is no longer the food of choice for people. So we don't stop to examine that particular assumption. Ironically, it's easier to try harder to do what used to work, than to acknowledge that times have changed.

Reflecting on the assumptions underlying what we do isn't easy. But it's essential for any church that wants to effectively live and proclaim the Gospel of Jesus in the 21st century.

Remember: People are Image Bearers.

People are created in the image of God. That may be one of the most startling things about Jesus' time in Samaria. The disciples know very well that humans are created in the image of God. For all of their differences, the Samaritans share the same Pentateuch, so the woman very likely believes the same thing. And yet, both cultures hold the other in contempt.

The biblical teaching that all humans are created in God's image is something we all agree with. At least in theory. But a quick scan of our social media accounts quickly proves that it's something we need to remember. Ed Stetzer laments: "Facebook is a cesspool of conspiracy theories, straw-man arguments, and schoolyard bullying. We have reached the point where the comment sections of major newspapers are a greater testament to the depravity of man than all the theology of the Reformers put together."[153] By way of illustration, he points to the 2015 Starbucks Red Cup controversy. That fall a man named Joshua Feuerstein posted on Facebook that "Starbucks REMOVED CHRISTMAS from their cups because they hate Jesus." It turns out that Feuerstein's accusations weren't true at all. Starbucks had never printed "Christmas" on its cups and had made no overt, or covert, attack on Christmas or Christianity. But instead of searching for truth; instead of responding with grace, Christians were outraged. Facebook, Twitter, and other social media outlets were inundated with angry responses from people who claim to follow Jesus. "You'd think," Stetzer says, "that someone had broken into churches and desecrated the altars if you looked at some Facebook feeds." People continued to buy coffee. Baristas continued to wish people "Merry Christmas" if they chose to do so. And the furor died away. But not before we Christians made ourselves look foolish and out of touch. Did we really think angry (and incorrect) diatribe would reflect positively on Jesus? Do we wonder why culture isn't interested in what we have to say?

Starbucks farce aside, there are undoubtedly plenty of corporations and individuals who say terrible things about Christians and about Christ. There may come a time when it's appropriate to assertively defend the reputation of Christ. But angry, disrespectful comments

183

are not the way to do it. In our interaction with the world around us (including with people within Jesus' ecclesia) we need to remember that all people were created in the image of God. That includes people we don't agree with.

As much attention as we do need to pay to our methods and witness, we must also keep in mind that the battle we are fighting is not essentially social, political, or physical. This is a spiritual fight and we're told more than once in Scripture that "the prayer of a righteous man is powerful and effective."[154] We often pray that the Lord will turn our nation back to him. We usually mean the nation as a political entity. That's not a bad thing, but what we should be praying is that God would turn people to him. As we purposely keep in mind that all people are created in his image, we'll be more likely to remember that all people are broken and in need of Jesus. When we think of those we encounter as hurting, lost people created in the image of God but separated from him, we're much more likely to interact with them in a way that is restorative, honoring, and will lower rather than raise barriers.

Relearn: Understand Culture

Jesus, not surprisingly, seems to understand the Samaritan culture. He's fully versed in what the woman's cultural assumptions are and is fully able to engage in conversation that uses her own culture as the starting point. As a side note, it's a beautiful thing to follow the course of their conversation and realize that Jesus adroitly moves cups of water to general spiritual topics to very specific issues in the woman's life. Never once does he denigrate her beliefs or statements. He simply, graciously redirects conversation. The disciples, on the other hand, don't seem to quite get it. When they join Jesus, they are surprised to find him stepping so far outside their cultural expectations, but they are at a loss as to why that might be the case. "No one asks, 'What do you want?' or 'Why are you talking with her?'"[155] It seems obvious that part of their reluctance to ask such questions is because they trust that Jesus knows what he's doing. Perhaps less obviously, they're also totally out of their element. Jewish men simply do not trek through Samaria, engage in conversation with a woman, and then drink from her cup. It would take the early church, steeped in Jewish culture, a long time to come to grips with how to interact with the non-Jewish culture around them

Like the disciples, we find ourselves totally out of our element as we try to engage with a society that seems to have changed without telling us. And so we fall back to what we know: trying to draw people to church so they can encounter Christ. But if we ask "how can we make our church more attractive to the unchurched" we have already lost our way. Our church doesn't matter. The real question is, "how can we help people see how attractive Jesus is?" And the answer to that question is going to be different, at least in part, in the 21st century than it was in the 20th. Certainly, part of the answer is in the way we experience and express what it means to be the Community of the Gospel. That part has not and will not change. Interestingly, as culture places an increasingly high value on things like the journey, the experience, and relationships, we're perfectly positioned to embrace those things which are already deeply meaningful to the people around us. If only we can move past our own history of individualism and embrace ecclesia as described in the New Testament.

In order to answer that question ("how can we help people see how attractive Jesus is?"); in order to fully engage society as Jesus instructed, the church needs to relearn what we think we know about the society we live in. "Our understanding of the message is so embedded in a white, Eurocentric, post-Reformation view of the gospel," explains Livermore.[156] That's not to say that everything we think we know is wrong. But for the most part, the world around us is rejecting that white, Eurocentric, post-Reformation paradigm. We need to understand the culture in which we live so that we can articulate the Gospel in a way that makes sense in the culture of the 21st century.

Much of this book has been something of a primer on that topic. But we've barely scratched the surface of culture in general. We've not even tried to consider the unique cultural context we each live in. One great option is for churches to create a team (or teams) which will dive deeply into issues and needs of their local culture, bringing their report and recommendations back to the church. There are so many things to consider. For example, what are the demographics of your area? Are you in an area with lots of young people? Or is your church in a retirement community? Is poverty a major concern? You might want to find ways to be involved in the poverty alleviation efforts of your town. Or are people trying to figure out how to handle enormous wealth? Chances are, the community is already trying to deal with these things and the church simply needs to join in.

What are the key social concerns in your community? I mentioned earlier that in my county, youth drug abuse and mental health problems are above national norms. One of the reasons I got involved was precisely because this is one of the most pressing issues in my area. With over 60 different organizations involved in that particular nonprofit coalition, not only do I have the opportunity to address a real need, I also get to be involved with dozens of people who may never walk into my church.

You might also discover current fads and trends. Is your community all about sports? I attended a church near Pittsburg, Pennsylvania a few years ago. Pittsburg is Steeler Nation (that's football, for the few readers who aren't familiar with that nomenclature). People attended church decked out in their Steeler colors. I haven't seen anything quite like it anywhere else. So our church did everything it could to intentionally be involved in the things that mattered to our community. Maybe in your city the fad isn't quite as positive. Maybe your area is ground zero for vaping, or alcoholism, or something else. As your team identifies the trends, consider how the church can get involved in positive ways.

You might also create a team to tackle the issues of holy living in the church's current environment. For example, without falling into the pharisaical trap of legalism, how can business people, counselors, teachers, pilots, financiers, farmers live holy lives in their spheres of influence and pressure? If your community has some pronounced negative thing happening (like the youth mental health issues facing my community), that issue is likely having a strong impact on your own church. Our youth ministry team regularly tackles issues like cutting (a horrible part of our town's youth culture) and gender identification (another major issue our local culture struggles with).

Whatever the issues facing your unique community, you won't be able to address them until you have a better understanding of what they are.

Relate: Build Relationships of Trust

Years ago someone taught me to listen for echoes. In other words, whether I'm leading, studying, or trying to understand culture, I try to listen for themes that repeat, concepts that keep popping up, or phrases that just stick in my head. Throughout my study of both Jesus' church and 21st century culture, "relationships" is one of those echoes. Time and time again the New Testament reminds us that the church is about relationships. We're known as Jesus' followers by the love we show each other (that requires being together). We're told to love one another, pray for one another, care for one another, carry one another's burdens, and hold one another accountable. All that requires being in relationships that transcend what happens in a worship service on the weekend.

Similarly, culture is all about relationships. That's a bit ironic given the strong component of neo-individualism, but there you have it. People value relationship over institution just about every time. Neo-individualism claims we're each on a journey toward personal authenticity, but it requires the validation of others. Justice is paramount, but for justice to even be a thing, you need people, plural. Research on spiritual growth also echoes the theme. While content acquisition happens best in a lecture, life transformation happens best in small groups of people in trusting relationships. The echo is persistent and the implication clear. As the church, we must "shift our understanding of church from an institution to a relational community."[157]

In the 21st century it's all about building relationships of trust. That's pretty much what we see Jesus doing at the well. Think about it. The disciples have all gone into the town to pick up some lunch. It isn't that far, and it's hard to imagine that Jesus is so tired that he simply can't keep going. But he chooses to stay behind, presumably so he can meet the woman. As we follow the conversation it's easy to see Jesus beginning to develop a relationship. It's a relatively quick conversation, but we learn later that Jesus stayed in the town for two more days.[158] Can you imagine what must be going through the disciples' minds as Jesus tells them to find a hotel for a couple of days? It's bad enough that they're traveling through the area, talking to women, drinking from their cups, now they have to stay there? Developing relationships isn't easy, particularly when we're intentionally following Jesus' example and building those relationships with people from another culture. We can't just blow through town dropping "Jesus saves" leaflets out the window. Developing relationships takes both time and proximity. We have to go where people live, drink from their cups, share their lives, stay in their town.

Rather than finding ways to attract more people to "church" to be ministered to by the professional staff, we need to be following Jesus' mandate to "go make disciples." In a culture that is cynical about institutions and distrustful of anyone who claims to have the "answers," the church needs to get "out there" and be involved in our communities. We need to be a gracious, godly presence in the activities that are important to those communities. There are unlimited opportunities to interact with people who are far from Christ; unlimited opportunities to pursue relationships of trust with those same people. And unlimited opportunities to represent Christ in those relationships. All of that not because we need a new tool in our church programming arsenal, but because it's at the heart of Jesus' mandate to his church.

Conclusion

After Christ's mandate for his people to go and make disciples, they did just that. They lived as the Community of the Gospel, proclaiming and living that Gospel in ways that were unmistakable to anyone who paid attention. They were "praising God and enjoying the favor of all the people. And the Lord added to their number daily those who were being saved."[159] At one point Peter and John were boldly telling people about Christ. The religious leaders "...were greatly disturbed because the apostles were teaching the people, proclaiming in Jesus the resurrection of the dead."[160] They had Peter and John arrested, but "When they saw the courage of Peter and John and realized that they were unschooled, ordinary men, they were astonished and they took note that these men had been with Jesus."[161]

The leaders realize that Peter and John are normal people living transformed lives. And they take note of the fact that these men are the way they are because they've been with Jesus. The leaders hated the message and railed against the Gospel, but they couldn't say anything bad about the resulting transformation. That's exactly what we're called to be and do. We're called to be so transformed as the Community of the Gospel that even when culture rejects the message of the Gospel, they can't argue with the transformation it brings.

When Jesus tells us that we will be his witnesses the statement is indicative not imperative. If you recall your high school language classes, you'll realize that we are not only directed to go and be witnesses (that's also a command we've already looked at), we are witnesses by virtue of our participation in Jesus' ecclesia. The question is not whether we will be witnesses. The question is what kind of witnesses we are. Sadly, much of the world sees no positive difference between the way Christians live and the way everyone else lives. The difference they do notice is that we stand opposed to many of the things they hold dear. And we don't seem to care about the things they care about.

As followers of Jesus, we must reclaim what it means to be his ecclesia, his Community of the Gospel. We must reflect on our own witness, examining assumptions behind what we do and why we do it. We must relearn what we think we know about a culture that has taken a radical shift in a very short amount of time. We must find ways to build authentic, trusting relationships with people outside our church bodies. We must be like the men of Issachar, understanding the times so that we will know what to do.

We're not told it will be easy, but Jesus does leave us with this assurance: "I have told you these things, so that in me you may have peace. In this world you will have trouble. But take heart! I have overcome the world."[162]

Now to him who is able to do immeasurably more than all
we ask or imagine,
according to his power that is at work within us,
to him be glory in the church and in Christ Jesus
throughout all generations,
for ever and ever! Amen.

Ephesians 3:20-21

Endnotes

[1] Root, Andrew. 2017. *Faith Formation in a Secular Age.* Grand Rapids, MI: Baker Academic, 98.

[2] Matthew 7:24-27

[3] Ephesians 1:17-19

[4] Matthew 16:13-20

[5] Matthew 16:23

[6] Matthew 16:16

[7] Matthew 16:17

[8] Matthew 16:18

[9] Matthew 16:19-20

[10] Matthew 16:19 (Williams New Testament)

[11] Matthew 18:18

[12] Acts 2:42-47

[13] 1 Peter 2:9-12

[14] Ephesians 1:4-5

[15] Exodus 19:6a

[16] 1 Peter 1:15-16

[17] Malachi 3:17

[18] Isaiah 43:18-21

[19] 1 Peter 2:12

[20] Arichea, D. C., & Nida, E. A. 1980. *A Handbook on the First Letter from Peter*. New York: United Bible Societies, 68-9.

[21] Matthew 16:1-3

[22] 1 Chronicles 11:1-3

[23] 1 Chronicles 12:23-38

[24] Luke 2:47

[25] Mark 12:32-33

[26] Colossians 1:9

[27] Judges 2:7

[28] Judges 2:10-11

[29] Daniel 2:19-23

[30] Colossians 1:9

[31] Sosnik, D. 2015. "American's Hinge Moment." *Politico,* March, 2015. https://www.politico.com/magazine/story/2015/03/2016-predictions-americas-sosnik-clinton-116480.

[32] Smith, K. 2015. "How a Massive Silent Cultural Revolution Has Changed America." *New York Post*, June 6, 2015. https://nypost.com/2015/06/06/how-a-massive-silent-cultural-revolution-has-changed-america/.

[33] Tickle, P. 2012. *The Great Emergence*. Grand Rapids, MI: Baker Books, 16.

[34] Jenkins, P. 2002. *The Next Christendom*. Oxford: Oxford University Press, 1.

[35] Tickle, P. 2012. *The Great Emergence*. Grand Rapids, MI: Baker Books, 14.

[36] *Christianity in its global context, 1900-2020.* 2013. South Hamilton, MA: Center for the Study of Global Christianity, 14.

[37] *Global Christianity: A Look at the Status of Christianity in 2018.* 2018. South Hamilton, MA: Center for the Study of Global Christianity.

[38] Pew Forum. 2015. "America's Changing Religious Landscape." *Pew Forum*, May 12, 2015. http://www.pewforum.org/2015/05/12/americas-changing-religious-landscape/.

[39] Granberg-Michaelson, Wesley. 2018. *Future Faith: Ten Challenges Reshaping Christianity in the 21st century*. Minneapolis, MN: Fortress Press. Kindle. 435.

[40] Jenkins, P. 2002. *The Next Christendom*. Oxford: Oxford University Press, 126-7.

[41] Granberg-Michaelson, Wesley. 2018. *Future Faith: Ten Challenges Reshaping Christianity in the 21st century*. Minneapolis, MN: Fortress Press. Kindle. 674.

[42] *Global Christianity: A Look at the Status of Christianity in 2018*. 2018. South Hamilton, MA: Center for the Study of Global Christianity. 76.

[43] Pew Research Center. 2018. "Origins and Destinations of the World's Migrants, 1990-2017." http://www.pewglobal.org/2018/02/28/global-migrant-stocks/?country=US&date=2017.

[44] *Global Christianity: A Look at the Status of Christianity in 2018*. 2018. South Hamilton, MA: Center for the Study of Global Christianity. 82.

[45] Granberg-Michaelson, Wesley. 2018. *Future Faith: Ten challenges reshaping Christianity in the 21st century*. Minneapolis, MN: Fortress Press. Kindle. 844.

[46] *Global Christianity: A Look at the Status of Christianity in 2018*. 2018. South Hamilton, MA: Center for the Study of Global Christianity. 83.

47 Wirzba, N. 2016. "Why we can now declare the end of 'Christian America.'" *Washington Post*, February 25, 2016. http://www.washingtonpost.com.

48 Hallowell, B. 2018. "'The First post-Christian Generation?': Skyrocketing Atheism Seen Among America's Teens." *Christian Broadcasting Network*, February 2, 2018. http://www1.cbn.com/cbnnews/2018/february/lsquo -the-first-post-christian-generation-rsquo- skyrocketing-atheism-seen-among-america-rsquo-s- teens.

49 Gilson, T. 2017. "Post-Christian no more: The western world has reinvented polytheism." *The Stream*, July 15, 2017. https://stream.org/post-christian-no-more- western-world-gods/.

50 Mohler, Albert. 2017. "The Advance of Secularism." *Ligonier Ministries*, March 1, 2017. https://www.ligonier.org/learn/articles/advance- secularism.

51 Barna Group. 2016. *Barna Trends 2017: What's New and What's Next at the Intersection of Faith and Culture.* Grand Rapids, MI: Baker Books, 156.

52 Barna Group. 2016. *Barna Trends 2017: What's New and What's Next at the Intersection of Faith and Culture.* Grand Rapids, MI: Baker Books, 139.

[53] Barna Group. 2016. *Barna Trends 2017: What's New and What's Next at the Intersection of Faith and Culture.* Grand Rapids, MI: Baker Books, 150.

[54] White, James E. 2017. *Meet Generation Z: Understanding and Reaching the New Post-Christian World.* Grand Rapids, MI: Baker Books, 28.

[55] Mohler, Albert. 2017. "The Advance of Secularism." *Ligonier Ministries*, March 1, 2017. https://www.ligonier.org/learn/articles/advance-secularism.

[56] Mohler, Albert. 2017. "The Advance of Secularism." *Ligonier Ministries*, March 1, 2017. https://www.ligonier.org/learn/articles/advance-secularism.

[57] White, James E. 2017. *Meet Generation Z: Understanding and Reaching the New Post-Christian World.* Grand Rapids, MI: Baker Books, 31.

[58] Dosmin, Barry, and Keysar, Ariela. 2008. *American Nones: The Profile of the No Religion Population.* Hartford, CT: Trinity College.

[59] White, James E. 2014. *The Rise of the Nones.* Grand Rapids, MI: Baker Books, 17.

[60] Daniel 1:1-8

[61] Daniel 1:18-21

[62] Daniel 6:10

[63] Livermore, David. 2009. *Cultural Intelligence: Improving Your CQ to Engage Our Multicultural World.* Grand Rapids, MI: Baker Academic, 169.

[64] Hiebert, Paul. (1994). *Anthropological Reflections on Missiological Issues.* Grand Rapids, MI: Baker Books, 115-6.

[65] Livermore, David. 2009. *Cultural Intelligence: Improving Your CQ to Engage Our Multicultural World.* Grand Rapids, MI: Baker Academic, 174.

[66] Baker, Mark. (no date) *Centered or Bounded?* www.discipleshipandethics.com/centered-or-bounded.

[67] Livermore, David. 2009. *Cultural Intelligence: Improving Your CQ to Engage Our Multicultural World.* Grand Rapids, MI: Baker Academic, 173.

[68] Daniel 6:25-28

[69] Joshua 11:23

[70] Joshua 24:24-27

[71] Judges 2:8-13

[72] I'm following the Barna Group's definitions of the generations since so much of their research has direct implications for the church.

[73] White, James E. 2017. *Meet Generation Z: Understanding and Reaching the new Post-Christian World*. Grand Rapids, MI: Baker Books, 47.

[74] White, James E. (2017). *Meet Generation Z: Understanding and Reaching the new Post-Christian World*. Grand Rapids, MI: Baker Books, 37.

[75] White, James E. 2017. *Meet Generation Z: Understanding and Reaching the new Post-Christian World*. Grand Rapids, MI: Baker Books, 11.

[76] Kane, Christy. 2018. "Electronics and the Brain." Lecture presented at the Utah Fall Substance Abuse Conference, Saint George, UT, September 19, 2018.

[77] Barna Group. 2016. *Barna Trends 2017: What's New and What's Next at the Intersection of Faith and Culture*. Grand Rapids, MI: Baker Books, 154.

[78] Root, Andrew. 2017. *Faith Formation in a Secular Age*. Grand Rapids, MI: Baker Academic, 486.

[79] Root, Andrew. 2017. *Faith Formation in a Secular Age*. Grand Rapids, MI: Baker Academic, 17.

[80] Root, Andrew. 2017. *Faith Formation in a Secular Age*. Grand Rapids, MI: Baker Academic, 6.

[81] Barna Group. 2016. *Barna Trends 2017: What's New and What's Next at the Intersection of Faith and Culture*. Grand Rapids, MI: Baker Books, 158.

[82] Kinnaman, David. 2007. *Unchristian: What a New Generation Really Thinks About Christianity...and Why It Matters.* Grand Rapids, MI: Baker Books, 44.

[83] Kinnaman, David. 2007. *Unchristian: What a New Generation Really Thinks About Christianity...and Why It Matters.* Grand Rapids, MI: Baker Books, 55-56.

[84] Cole, Neil. 2010. *Church 3.0: Upgrades for the Future of the Church.* San Francisco, CA: Wiley, 40.

[85] Cole, Neil. 2010. *Church 3.0: Upgrades for the Future of the Church.* San Francisco, CA: Wiley, 23.

[86] White, James. 2018. "Colleges are Changing for Generation." *Church and Culture* (blog). August 30, 2018, https://www.churchandculture.org/blog/2018/8/30/colleges-are-changing-for-generation-z.

[87] Hosea 12:6

[88] Zechariah 7:9-10

[89] Micah 2:1-2

[90] Micah 6:6-7

[91] Micah 6:8

[92] Barna Group. 2017. *Barna trends 2018: The Truth about a Post-Truth Society.* Grand Rapids, MI: Baker Books, 73.

[93] Barna Group. 2016. *Barna Trends 2017: What's New and What's Next at the Intersection of Faith and Culture.* Grand Rapids, MI: Baker Books, 154.

[94] Barna Group. 2016. *Barna Trends 2017: What's New and Next at the Intersection of Faith and Culture.* Grand Rapids, MI: Baker Books, 45.

[95] Barna Group. 2016. *Barna Trends 2017: What's New and Next at the Intersection of Faith and Culture.* Grand Rapids, MI: Baker Books, 46.

[96] Barna Group. 2016. *Barna Trends 2017: What's New and Next at the Intersection of Faith and Culture.* Grand Rapids, MI: Baker Books, 47.

[97] Barna Group. 2016. *Barna Trends 2017: What's New and Next at the Intersection of Faith and Culture.* Grand Rapids, MI: Baker Books, 161.

[98] Matthew 6:3

[99] White, James E. 2017. *Meet Generation Z: Understanding and Reaching the New Post-Christian World.* Grand Rapids, MI: Baker Books, 19.

[100] Harari, Uval Noah. 2017. *Homo Deus: A Brief History of Tomorrow.* New York, NY: Harper, 292-93.

[101] Yarhouse, Mark. 2015. "Understanding the Transgender Phenomenon." *Christianity Today*, June 8, 2015. www.christianitytoday.com/ct/2015/july-

august/understanding-transgender-gender-dysphoria.html.

[102] Barna Group. 2016. *Barna Trends 2017: What's New and Next at the Intersection of Faith and Culture.* Grand Rapids, MI: Baker Books, 14.

[103] Wirzba, Norman. 2015. *From Nature to Creation.* Grand Rapids, MI: Baker Academic, 86-7.

[104] Wirzba, Norman. 2018. "Opinion: Can we live in a world without a Sabbath? Rethinking the human in the Anthropocene." *Australian Broadcasting Corporation*, November 29, 2018. https://www.abc.net.au/religion/rethinking-the-human-in-the-anthropocene/10567192.

[105] Genesis 1:28-29

[106] Genesis 2:15

[107] Cory Maxwell-Coghlan. 2016. "Are Humans Responsible for Global Warming?" *The Barna Group*, September 22, 2016. https://www.barna.com/research/humans-responsible-global-warming/.

[108] Psalm 37:4

[109] Stetzer, Ed. 2018. *Christians in the Age of Outrage: How to Bring Our Best When the World is at Its Worst.* Carol Stream, IL: Tyndale House Publishers 2018. Kindle, loc 2658.

[110] Acts 2:11-12

[111] Acts 2:36

[112] Acts 2:42-47

[113] Matthew 28:20

[114] Polhill, J. B. 1992. *Acts* (Vol. 26). Nashville: Broadman & Holman Publishers, 119-20.

[115] Boice, James Montgomery. *Acts: An Expositional Commentary*. 1997. Grand Rapids, MI: Baker Books, Acts 58-9.

[116] Newman, B. M., and Nida, E. A. 1972. *A Handbook on the Acts of the Apostles*. New York: United Bible Societies, 62-3.

[117] Newman, B. M., and Nida, E. A. 1972. *A Handbook on the Acts of the Apostles*. New York: United Bible Societies, 62-3.

[118] Acts 4:31

[119] Acts 4:32-35

[120] Shatte, Andrew. 2018. "The Resilience Factor." Lecture presented at the Utah Fall Substance Abuse Conference, Saint George, UT, September 19, 2018.

[121] Ephesians 4:11-13

[122] Creasy Dean, Kenda. 2010. *Almost Christian: What the Faith of Our Teenagers Is Telling the American Church.* Oxford, NY: Oxford University Press, 11.

[123] Ritch, David. 2016. *Faithful Presence: Seven Disciplines That Shape the Church for Mission.* Downers Grove: IL, IVP Books, 9.

[124] Acts 2:42-47

[125] John 13:34-35

[126] Block, Peter. 2008. *Community: The Structure of Belonging.* San Francisco, CA Berrett-Koehler Publishers, 25.

[127] Ephesians 4:11-13

[128] Matthew 28:18-20

[129] Luke 6:40

[130] Barna Group. 2016. *Barna Trends 2017: What's New and Next at the Intersection of Faith and Culture.* Grand Rapids, MI: Baker Books, 159.

[131] Barna Group. 2016. *Barna Trends 2017: What's New and Next at the Intersection of Faith and Culture.* Grand Rapids, MI: Baker Books, 157.

[132] Psalm 71:18

[133] Psalm 145:4

[134] Titus 2:2-4

[135] 1 Peter 3:15

[136] Acts 17:16-23

[137] 1 Corinthians 9:22-3

[138] Stetzer, Ed. 2018. *Christians in the Age of Outrage: How to Bring Our Best When the World is at Its Worst.* Carol Stream, IL: Tyndale House Publishers 2018. Kindle, loc 2745.

[139] Philippians 4:8

[140] Stetzer, Ed. 2018. *Christians in the Age of Outrage: How to Bring Our Best When the World is at Its Worst.* Carol Stream, IL: Tyndale House Publishers 2018. Kindle, loc 2833.

[141] John 4:35

[142] 2 Corinthians 2:14-16

[143] Nye, Chris. 2015. "Leading the 21st Century Church." *Christianity Today*, June 4, 2015. https://www.christianitytoday.com/pastors/2015/june-web-exclusives/leading-21st-century-church.html.

[144] Cole, Neil. 2010. *Church 3.0: Upgrades for the Future of the Church.* San Francisco, CA: Wiley, 22.

[145] Isaiah 43:19

[146] Barna Group. 2014. "Five Trends Among the Unchurched." *The Barna Group*, October 9, 2014. https://www.barna.com/research/five-trends-among-the-unchurched/.

[147] Matthew 28:18-20

[148] Mark 16:15

[149] John 20:21

[150] John 4:4-26

[151] John 4:39

[152] John 4:27

[153] Stetzer, Ed. 2018. *Christians in the Age of Outrage: How to Bring Our Best When the World is at Its Worst.* Carol Stream, IL: Tyndale House Publishers 2018. Kindle, loc 303.

[154] James 5:16

[155] John 4:27

[156] Livermore, David. *Cultural Intelligence: Improving Your CQ to Engage Our Multicultural World.* Baker Academic, 2009, p. 194.

[157] Cole, Neil. 2010. *Church 3.0: Upgrades for the Future of the Church.* San Francisco, CA: Wiley, 30.

[158] John 4:40

[159] Acts 2:47

[160] Acts 4:2

[161] Acts 4:13

[162] John 16:33

Also by Steve White

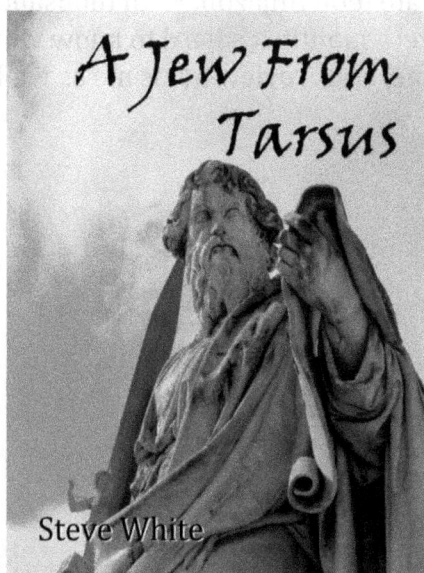

Alternately described as a terrorist, author, teacher, mentor, and heretic, the Apostle Paul is arguably one of the most influential figures in history. Bursting onto the stage of the first century Roman Empire, Paul brings together Roman, Greek and Hebrew cultures in his own unique fashion. At the heart of his message was the "musterion" – the revealed mystery. Namely, that in the fullness of time God had revealed his plan to rescue and redeem humanity – all humanity. Whether welcomed or cursed, beaten or blessed, Paul was never ignored. And his message changed the world.

Available on Amazon

Thanks for reading *Shift: Church in the 21st Century*. If you found it helpful, please take a few more minutes to review and rate it on Amazon. With thousands of books published every month, it's hard to know which are worth the time. Your review helps me as well as others.

www.ingramcontent.com/pod-product-compliance
Lightning Source LLC
Chambersburg PA
CBHW050115280326
41933CB00010B/1112